REALTOR'S TOP SECRETS

Practical Tips to Buying and Selling a Home That Your Realtor Hasn't Told You

JOHN KAUFMAN

FOREWORD

One of the most expensive, most complicated and important financial decisions we make in our lives is buying and selling a home. Not only is your home likely the largest single purchase and investment that most of us ever make in our lives, it's also one of the most stressful.

———

As a realtor I have been fortunate enough to assist many people through the process and have made some lifelong friends as a result. I am writing this book because one of the things I find myself doing as a realtor is educating people on the process while in the middle of the process. Not having information and experience is what leads to stress as a buyer or seller, and suddenly being thrown into the process of mortgages, title companies, offers, counter offers, earnest money, appraisals and inspections can be confusing for anyone. The first exposure that most people have with any of it is when they begin buying or selling a home, and hopefully they are being guided by a knowledgable, helpful realtor that has their best interests in mind.

———

I hope that the information I am giving you in this book will help guide you and make the process go smoother, and with less stress. If you are in Northeast Ohio in one of the markets I service I would be glad to help you personally, and if I can't or I'm not the right fit for you, I'll be more than happy to assist you by referring you to an experienced realtor to help you.

———

One last note, this book is not perfect or all encompassing. It is going to have a few spelling or grammatical errors, because I personally wrote it in my spare time late in the evenings in order to have something of value to provide to my potential clients. If you find errors, have suggestions for things that could be added, would like my help finding you a pre-screened realtor nationwide or simply want help buying or selling a home in Northeast Ohio, please feel free to contact me any time at:

———

www.JohnKaufmanRealEstate.com
  www.ohiohomevalues.info
    jKaufmanRE@gmail.com

———

Thanks,
   John Kaufman

Chapter One

YOU'VE DECIDED TO MOVE

When you first decide to sell your home, many decisions need to be made and the consequences of these decisions are long lasting.

———

One of the first steps most homeowners take is starting the search for a new home, because of course, searching for a new home is not only fun, but it's giving you a glimpse of what your future life will be like. And there are a lot of considerations that need to be made when searching for a new home as well, but the focus of this book is to help you understand the process of both buying a new home as well as selling your existing home efficiently, profitably, and in a way that helps you move forward with your future.

Chapter Two

PREPARING YOUR HOME FOR SALE

Preparing Your Home for Sale

———

Like anything that you want to do right, selling a home goes easier if you are prepared ahead of time. As a realtor I help people through this process and hopefully some of the lessons that I've learned along the way can help make this experience go smoothly for you.

———

If you know you are going to be selling your home well in advance, I always recommend preparing for it so that you'll be able to sell your home quickly for a fair price. Some basic steps I recommend to prepare your home for sale are:

———

- Give your home a thorough cleaning. When we

live in a home for years, we tend to become blind to the sights and smells of our own home.

- Have carpets and floors professionally cleaned
- Walls and paint should ideally be fresh and clean
- Rooms should be free of clutter
- Landscaping should be neat, overgrowth trimmed, unhealthy trees etc... removed
- Catch up on small repairs that you've been putting off
- Consider pressure washing the outside and any concrete or paved driveways
- Decks, railings, trim should be freshly painted, loose boards tightened etc...

———

Basically go through your home and fix or have fixed and cleaned up anything obvious that someone viewing the home for the first time might see that would cause them to believe that the home has not been well maintained.

———

When buyers visit your home you only have one chance to make a good first impression, and nothing generates offers more quickly than a fresh, clean, well maintained low maintenance home that looks "loved". Buyers are notorious for deducting thousands of dollars from offers over issues that could have been fixed with a $20 can of paint. Preparing early will keep money in your pocket in the end.

———

If you want to sell your home quickly for full value you must think like a buyer

———

Buyers search for homes several ways:

- Online – real estate sites like realtor.com, Zillow, Brokerage websites
- Yard Signs – Driving neighborhoods they're interested in
- Online Classifieds – Craigslist, Facebook, etc…
- Referrals – Someone they know saw a place and told them about it
- Working with a Realtor – they have a "Buyer's Agent" assisting and representing their interests

———

When searching for a home buyers are typically looking for a home that fits their needs, looks good, has the right location, and is the right size with the right features. Finding a home online is a very visual process, and even when working with a buyer's agent they will usually be seeing a home that their agent has e-mailed to them and the photo's of that home will make the first impression that will result in them scheduling a time to see the property. Clean, modern, well maintained homes simply generate more showings resulting in more offers faster for the seller.

———

Buyers look at homes specifically to see how a home fits their needs, and they tend to be very unemotional about most of the homes they view. They may like the location, the size, the layout, and just hate the color of the carpet in the second guest bedroom which leads them to keep looking instead of making an offer. Buyers tend to look at a home in its "present condition" overlooking its "potential". Small things like not liking the wallpaper in the basement bathroom can become a dealbreaker to a buyer even though it could be changed to their liking easily and inexpensively.

———

As a seller you have no control over your location, you have no control over the size and shape of your home, your neighbors, or how many bedrooms and bathrooms your home has but pay attention to your home through the critical eyes of a buyer and you can understand the feedback you'll get later.

———

To Repair or Not Repair - That is the Question

———

When it comes to making repairs in advance of selling a home it's really a judgement call. You have to consider the value of the home, the cost of the repair, the severity of not making the repair, and your financial ability to make the repair.

———

I'll go back to a personal experience from a couple of years back. I had a client that was selling a home that they knew had something wrong with the septic system. Now the fear with septic systems is that the repair could cost $20,000 and the seller just didn't want to risk that because she couldn't afford the repairs if they ran that high. She chose instead to disclose that there was an issue with the septic and that she would fix it after the sale through escrow funds.

———

Dozens of buyers went through the home, and several mentioned that the reason that they didn't make an offer was the uncertainty with the septic tank. Even though the seller would fix it after the sale, they just didn't want to risk it. Finally after months of waiting a buyer came along and made an offer on the home, and lowballed over $10,000 directly due to the septic issue and STILL required the seller to pay the repairs. The extra $10,000 was "just in case,", and this was the best offer on the table. The seller accepted the offer, and when the septic repair company came to fix it, they found out that it was a $25 piece of plastic that needed replaced with a total repair bill of only $250. Had the seller fixed the septic prior to listing it would have cost her $250, saved months of showings and netted her at LEAST $10,000 more on the sale of the house.

———

I had another home that I was assisting a buyer with that had an in-ground pool. The seller disclosed that the pool needed around $5,000 worth of maintenance to repair a small crack and reseal the pool that she didn't want to do prior to the sale. My buyers loved the home, and actually wanted to put an offer input the thought of not knowing 100% for sure what was going on with the pool scared them off. What it it would really cost $6,000? $60,000? My buyers weren't experts on unground pools or the costs to maintain them, the unknown nature of the repair cost became a major hurdle to them an eventually they bought a house that didn't have a pool at all. There were also a few other small things like a kitchen cabinet door that was missing a handle (probably a $20 fix in an almost $400,000 home). I showed this home several times for different buyers during it's time on the market and when the home eventually sold after staying on the market for over a year it sold for over $20,000 less than my first buyers were interested in it for.

––––––

The moral of this story is if the buyer sees something that needs fixed, it's usually cheaper to have it fixed than to negotiate about fixing it IF they don't just move on to another house that doesn't require repairs, or will make an offer that is extremely low in order to protect themselves as the buyer. I've been involved with a lot of investors who fix and flip houses over the years and have done some of that myself. I have a basic idea of repair costs, but the majority of buyers don't because they are buying a house to live in it not to work on it. The common thing you hear from a buyer is, "It'll take $50,000 to fix the problems with this house," when it will probably take $500 to fix everything they think needs fixed. If you can help it don't lose sales or money by ignoring the small repairs that you can have done in advance.

––––––

Upgrades

––––––

Besides repairs, upgrades are another hot issue when selling a home. Is now the time to remodel the kitchen? Redo the bathrooms? The answer is "maybe".......

———

I have worked with a lot of house flippers over the years and they make money by fixing up and modernizing homes that have fallen into disrepair and reselling them at a profit. Freshly remodeled homes are usually the top sellers. A new kitchen and bath, can make your home the most in demand hope on the market So the question is should you "flip your own home"?

———

In some cases yes, but in most cases probably not. If you kitchen looks like a war zone, cracked 50 year old formica, worn out floors, etc... then the cost of a cheap upgrade will probably be worth it. Just having it look clean, new and maintained could put your home ahead of the competition on the market. Just be careful not to over improve because you can't charge more than the comparable homes on the market even if it's nicer. So if the neighbors houses all have formica, it probably won't pay to upgrade to granite. In these cases, painting, cleaning, and upgrading inexpensive things that "show" may be the way to go.

———

Upgrades are really a house by house decision. Consult your contractor for cost, and your realtor or appraiser can give an opinion on post upgrade market value.

———

———

Prepare Your Landscaping

———

When it comes to landscaping, neat, clean, low maintenance usually wins the day. Get rid of overgrowth - trees, shrubs, bushes etc... that block views of the home, and fallen branches, and leaves that give an unkept look to the yard. The #1 rule is get rid of overgrowth and put down fresh mulch in your flower beds.

———

Few things can change a home's curb appeal like neat clean fresh landscaping. This is one priority that should be high in your pre-sale prep.

———

Decluttering

———

When we live in our homes we all collect clutter. From extra bottles in the shower, to papers on the countertop, and those clothes that we haven't worn in years that are hanging in the closet.

———

Buyers looking at a house are turned off by clutter. If you want your home to sell I recommend boxing up extra out of season clothes, paperwork you don't need, the kids extra toys, and anything that tends to be "left out" but you really can live without for a while. When you de-clutter your house will look bigger and roomier, and more inviting for the buyer. This leads to faster sales for more money. Typically the investment into a storage unit for a month or two is small compared to the perception of a roomy clean, low maintenance house with ample storage.

———

Kids toys laying around, dirty clothes on the floor, dirty dishes in the sink, anything that looks out of place can potentially turn off buyers. Just make sure that the house is neat and clean, and ready to be shown on short notice. I know this is an inconvenience for many sellers, but the better job you do at this up front will lead to a faster sale and you won't have to keep this routine up for nearly as long.

———

Depersonalizing

———

This one is hard for people sometimes, but it's something I highly recommend. Depersonalizing a home means taking down some of the family photo's vacation pics, unique decorations that are relevant only to you. Don't worry, you can put them all back up in your new home. The reason realtors recommend doing this is that we want the buyer to walk into your beautiful home and visualize their own life fitting into the home. Buyer's may to be taken out of that experience if they see photos of the current occupants, etc and start visualizing you living in your home instead of them. So by all means keep it decorated, lived in, and loved, just remember that while it's on the market keep it ready for the customer to feel equally at home because with any luck they'll want to call it home.

———

Should You Get an Inspection Prior to Listing Your Home?

———

If you can afford to, I recommend getting a general inspection prior to listing your home for sale. This gives you the opportunity to address any issues with the home, have them fixed and provide buyer's agents as well as buyers with the security of knowing that you have nothing to hide, and that you have pro-actively fixed known issues beforehand.

———

A qualified inspector can uncover potential roadblocks to selling your home that your buyer is going to uncover anyway when they hire an inspector prior to closing, and then they'll likely use their inspection to ask for concessions from you as a seller either in the form of getting the issues repaired or money taken off the selling price and out of your pocket. In many cases if you have a recent inspection report and receipts showing that the recommended repairs have already been made a buyer may even choose not to have their own inspection performed because they have a higher level of confidence in your home vs others on the market.

———

This can raise the perceived value of your home in the buyer's mind, and lead to a much smoother closing process and sometimes higher offers from the buyer. If you had the choice of making an offer on two equivalent homes, one that already had an inspection and all major issues addressed prior to you viewing the home in the first place, and a home that you will have to pay for an inspection on and negotiate with the seller on what repairs they are willing to do if any, which would you choose? Your buyer will be making the same judgement in their minds.

———

Should you market your home while living in it or when it's vacant?

———

Sometimes when relocating, in estate sales, divorces, or other situations you may find yourself faced with the question of marketing your home empty vs still living in it. Each way has its own benefits and drawbacks and I'll discuss them here.

———

Selling while occupied is the most common situation, and much of the advice I've given such as decluttering, depersonalizing, and fixing minor things applies to this situation. The advantage of marketing the home while occupied is that the home looks lived in, and the buyers seeing your furniture in the rooms, your clothes hanging in the closet, and even some food in the pantry gives them a sense of what the home would be like to live in it. It also gives them a good sense of scale and how their furniture and family may fit in the home after they buy it. The drawback is that you'll be keeping the home showing ready, and have to leave when people are coming to look, and have to deal with the issues that go along with that.

————

Selling while vacant on the other hand has the advantage of being easier on the seller because you clean it once, and the home can be shown anytime because agents can schedule for an immediate showing without worrying about your schedule as a seller. No sick kids, birthday parties, or Sunday football games to be interrupted or sales missed out on because you just had no way to let people view the home when they were available. It also has the disadvantage of the home looking empty, cold, and impersonal if it has no furniture, and has been completely moved out of. This can lead to longer time on the market, lower offers, and lower perceived value in general because the buyer is now looking at that one weird spot on the living room wall with a 1/8 inch dimple that would never be seen if there were furniture in the room. They also can't see how their furniture might fit, and the bedroom looks small because they're SURE that their bed might not fit (even though your bedroom is a foot longer and wider than the one they have now).

————

So you already moved out and your home is vacant. How can

you inexpensively stage it for sale? There are staging companies in most cities that will rent you furniture and professionally decorate your home with furniture that matches and makes the home look not only lived in but professionally decorated. Typically you don't have to fully furnish the entire home, but at a minimum I recommend putting furniture in the kitchen, living room, and master bedroom. These are the rooms that are likely very important to your buyers and often the most difficult for them to visualize their own furniture without a visual reference.

―――

The kitchen should have appliances, a refrigerator and a stove. Empty spaces mean the buyer is thinking about whether their refrigerator will fit, their stove will fit, and if they don't already have their own, how much it will cost to buy new, etc... (they probably will, but buyers are terrible at visualizing things) and having nice modern appliances there.

―――

If you don't have a staging company, how can you inexpensively furnish the home? One trick I learned from one of my clients that flips homes is... He will purchase used or scratch and dent stainless appliances for the kitchen and go to a pay by the month furniture store for some basic living room furniture such as a couch and kitchen table. He will sometimes only rent these long enough to have the home photographed or for an open house keeping the cost down yet giving him the benefit of having a home that looks furnished an ultimately sells quickly for more money. His initial investment is small compared to the amount he gets back.

Chapter Three

HOME VALUES

What determines a home's market value?

———

There is an old adage that there are three things that matter in real estate values.... Location, Location, and Location. Unfortunately it's slightly more complicated than that. In this section I'm not going to teach you enough to become a professional real estate appraiser, that is a very specialized field and is way beyond what most homeowners need. However, I can give you a high level overview that can hopefully take some of the mystery out of how "Market Value" is typically estimated by a realtor, a customer, and a lender.

———

Before we get started it's important to understand a few common terms we hear associated with home values.

———

1. Listing Price - This is the price that a home is offered for sale on the open market. This is the price you'll see online when viewing the home on websites like Zillow, Trulia, Realtor and in the MLS.

2. Tax Value - This is the county appraisal that your property taxes are based on

3. Selling Price - This is the price that a home actually sold for as recorded in the MLS and county records.

4. Appraisal - The statement of value that a licensed real estate appraiser has estimated that the property is worth on the open market.

5. Market Value - The most likely price that the home would sell for on the open market, in a reasonable timeframe in current conditions.

6. Zestimate - An estimate of market value provided from publicly available information scraped from the internet and compiled by Zillow

7. Realist Estimate - A tool used by licensed realtors to estimate market value using actual contracted selling prices of comparable homes within the MLS.

8. CMA - Comparative Market Analysts - a report compiled by a licensed realtor comparing a subject home with other recent sales, as well as current homes on the market to estimate the homes likely market value in the current market. This combines data, market knowledge and experience to arrive at the value estimate. This method is significantly more accurate than automated methods or tax estimates when performed by an experienced realtor, second only to a full appraisal.

9. Replacement Cost - The cost to tear down and

replace the structures on the property in event of disaster

10. Loan to Value Ratio (LTV) - The LTV determines the amount of money a buyer can borrow in order to purchase a home. This ratio depends on the type of loan the buyer is using to finance with FHA, VA, and Conventional loans having different LTV ratios. They are typically used to protect the bank in case the buyer defaults on the loan. A buyer can typically only buy a home that costs more than the LTV will support if they bring extra cash to the table, and it serves as a ceiling on the amount that a home can reasonably be expected to sell for.

11. Equity - The difference between what is owed on the mortgage, and the market value of the property.

12. Over Improved - This is the term you'll hear when you see that $100,000 market value home with a $50,000 deck, $20,000 in landscaping, marble floors, high end fixtures, and the best of everything throughout. I'll include a section on this later in this chapter.

———

Few things are more controversial and cause more friction between a seller and a realtor than how to price a home.

———

To understand why this is, we have to look at what each party in a home sale / purchase wants....

————

The seller wants to get as much money for their home as quickly as possible, while spending as little as possible to get it. The seller wants to have as much money left after paying off their mortgage as possible so that they can invest the money into their next home or their retirement, education, family, etc... This means that sellers will often over-estimate the market value of their home, and stick to that because they overpaid initially, over improved, have second or third mortgages, etc... that prevent them from selling at fair market value.

————

The listing agent wants to get a fair price for his client, collect a fair commission for his efforts and to treat both the seller and the buyer fairly and ethically. A realtor spends time and money helping a seller sell their home and ONLY gets paid if and when the home successfully sells. A reputable, experienced realtor will typically refuse to list a home that is priced significantly above market value without assurances from the seller that the home will be priced fairly before the listing agreement is finished. Less experienced realtors often make unrealistic promises to sellers in order to fill their listing pipeline and generate buyer leads that will purchase other homes in the neighborhood. Sellers often think that realtors guiding a price lower is a selfish move by the realtor, however there are many times as a realtor we guide our clients higher as well. An honest realtor will give an honest opinion of market value regardless of the situation because we have an obligation to be fair and honest.

————

The buyer, wants to pay as little for the new home so that they aren't wasting money, and they are fearful of being taken advantage of, missing unnoticed defects in the property that will cost them money later or simply overpaying for the home. A buyer will almost never pay more for house X than they would for house Y if they are reasonably similar. If house X is priced $10,000 more than house Y and Z and they are all significantly similar the buyer will view house X as over priced and choose a similar option for less money, or offer the seller the same price they would for one of the other options. Essentially house X is helping houses Y & Z sell faster while sitting on the market until all of the similar homes have sold. The buyer's agent wants to

––––––

The buyer's agent wants to get their client a fair deal, while protecting their client from harm. They also have an obligation to treat the all parties in the sale honestly and ethically. While the agent could theoretically make more money in commission by encouraging their client to bid higher on a home they have an ethical obligation to advise their client regarding the fair market value and allow the client to make their own bidding decisions based on that information. Guiding the price higher for personal gain would violate the agents ethical duty to protect their client's best interest over their own. This means that buyer's agents guide their buyers based on comparable recent sales and expected market values, not a desired commission amount.

––––––

The lender wants to successfully make a loan and protect their bank from loss. This means that they will only loan based on the allowable loan to value (LTV) ratios for the loan type. Conventional mortgages have higher LTV ratios than FHA, VA, etc... loans. There are many laws regulating these ratios, and the lender's obligations which were made significantly stricter after the housing crisis in 2008/2009. The bank can only loan based on the value determined by an independent 3rd party appraiser who's job it is to look at homes and compare them to the market and protect the banks by not allowing them to lend too much for a home that cannot reliably be resold for as much as they lent on it.

———

Next we will explore each of these perspectives in greater detail.

FROM A SELLER'S POINT OF VIEW

Home Values from the Seller's Point of View

As a seller we all naturally want to get the most money possibly out of your home. One of the great fears we all have when selling a home is that we might not get the full value out of our home. We saw the neighbor's house sell for $_____ last month, and we obviously think our own house is better than the neighbor's house, and therefore should sell for even more money, so we insist on pricing it 10% higher than that house based on that feeling.

In actual practice however, we have to compare our house to our neighbor's house the way a bank appraiser, and our eventual customers will in order to get a realistic real world estimate of the fair market value. The best way to do that is to hire a licensed appraiser (the same people the banks use to determine the lendable value of the home later). The best FREE way to do this is to ask a qualified realtor to perform a CMA on your home and give you an estimated market value.

———

Things that we believe positively affect market value as owners

- Higher quality landscaping
- Larger deck
- More expensive fixtures / finishes
- Extensive improvements beyond anything the neighbor's have
- Personal flourishes / DIY projects that are specific to this home and special to the owner.

———

———

Home Values from the Buyer's Point of View

FROM A BUYER'S POINT OF VIEW

———

As a buyer we all naturally want to get the most home possible for the least amount of money. One of the great fears we all have when buying a home is that we might overpay for our home. We saw the neighbor's house sell for $_____ last month, in the neighborhood where we found the house we like, and we obviously think our prospective house is roughly the same as the neighbor's house, and therefore should sell for about the same money, so we insist on offering 10% lower than that house based on that feeling so that we don't overpay.

———

In actual practice however, we have to compare our new prospective house to the neighbor's house the way a bank appraiser, and our eventual customers will in order to get a realistic real world estimate of the fair market value to guide our offer price. The best way to do that is to hire a licensed appraiser (the same people the banks use to determine the lendable value of the home later). The best FREE way to do this is to ask a qualified realtor to perform a CMA on your home and give you an estimated market value.

———

Things that we believe negatively affect market value as buyers

- Too much landscaping / maintenance
- Larger deck that is more than they actually need
- More expensive fixtures / finishes - will be expensive to replace or repair when needed
- Extensive improvements beyond anything the neighbor's have - buyer's kind of like these things, but many times won't want to stick out among the neighbors
- Personal flourishes / DIY projects that are specific to this home and special to the owner. - The buyer's tastes and needs may be different.

———

You'll notice that the very things that a seller believes support a higher selling price may be the same things that lower the perceived value to the buyer.

———

In general buyer's will pay for the "same" or "good enough" but they won't pay extra for things they didn't personally want in the first place. So that deck made out of material that cost 5X as much to build as the neighbor's is probably worth the same as the neighbor's to the buyer. It's even possible the buyer see the deck and wants to take it out and put in a stone patio instead.

————

The point is "Over-improving" your home beyond the standards of comparable homes may make your home sell faster at the same price as your neighbor's but it will very rarely result in it selling for more.

————

Home Values from the Realtor's Point of View

FROM A REALTOR'S POINT OF VIEW

―――――

As a realtor we all naturally want to get the most fair deal for both the seller and the buyer because we have a legal, ethical, and moral obligation to put our client's interests above our own. If we put a home on the market and it is significantly overpriced, or underpriced or it is marketed improperly we haven't helped the seller, the buyer, our broker, OR ourselves. We have let everyone down in that situation. This is one of the leading causes of homes being listed for months and the listings expiring with the home still unsold.

―――――

When a qualified realtor looks at the homes that recently sold and are currently for sale in your neighborhood, the realtor looks at the data and compares recent homes that have sold, homes currently on the market, and homes that were marketed that did not sell to your home.

————

Things that we believe affect market value as Realtors

- Recent home sale values of homes that are very similar to the house we are estimating market value for (ranch to ranch - split level to split level, etc...)
- Average days on the market for comparable homes
- Current number of comparable homes on the market and their asking prices
- Condition of property (finishes, fixtures, paint, etc...) compared to recent sales

————

The realtor's job is to look at the property through completely neutral eyes to determine through data and experience a likely selling price for the home in the current market using a combination of data, market knowledge and experience. A qualified realtor will sometimes determine that a home is worth more in the current market than the seller, will sometimes determine that it is worth less, or that the owner was initially correct, however the realtor should be arriving at the conclusion through work not guesses.

————

Home Values from the Lender's Point of View

FROM A LENDER'S POINT OF VIEW

A lender's job is to look at the value of a home from a safety perspective. In other words if the lender loans a buyer the money to purchase a home, and the buyer defaults on the loan, can the lender be reasonably expected to at least break even if the home is repossessed and re-sold.

If the lender lends too much money for a home they have lost the safety net that they need in order to comply with federal lending regulations, and they are putting their banks and the American economy at risk. How this plays out in real life is that the lender is willing to loan up to a predetermined % of the appraised value of the property.

For round numbers lets use a $250K home. If the lender is

able to lend on an 80% loan to value ratio then the buyer needs to have $50K down, and the lender will loan $200K pending appraisal.

———

If the bank's appraiser looks at the home, determines the value after doing an extremely through appraisal looking at the property from multiple perspectives, doing a LOT of calculations and turning in an appraisal that meets all legal guidelines and regulations that says that the home is worth exactly $250 then the deal goes through. If the appraiser says the home is worth $225K then the buyer is unlikely to be able to get a loan for the $200K they need in order to purchase the home. This sale will likely die unless the buyer comes up with an extra $25K, or the seller lowers the price enough to make the LTV work. If not, the home will have to go back out on the market at a lower price in order to know that the next buyer will be able to get financing with your likely buyers wondering what is "wrong" with your home since the listing went from "Contingent" to "Active"

———

This is the reason that KNOWING the likely realistic market value of your home as estimated by a qualified realtor, or appraiser BEFORE you put it on the market is so important.

———

———

Zillow "Zestimates"

ZILLOW "ZESTIMATES" & OTHER VALUATION TOOLS

———

One of the most popular features on Zillow is the "Zestimate" feature. It gives you an estimated home value right online without speaking to a realtor or feeling pressured in any way. It's a great service, and it can give you some ideas of the market trends, and recent pricing trends. However, Zillow and other online estimates are severely inaccurate and can be off by tens or even hundreds of thousands of dollars or more.

———

Why? Because automated online estimates are taking bulk data, and compiling and averaging it without local market knowledge, actual sales prices instead of asking prices, knowledge of the interior and exterior condition of the home, features, etc....

———

I had a personal experience with these estimates. A few years ago I decided to sell my home, and buy a new one. As a realtor I knew what the market value was of my home, but I wasn't in a hurry. The Zillow and other online estimates were showing my home at a value $50K higher than I thought it would bring based on my experience as a realtor. So I decided to try an experiment, and I listed my home for the Zillow Zestimate price. Over 6 months later my house's price had now been lowered OVER 50K and was finally under contract. I had used the old - better to start high because you can alway lower the price logic, and in the process I only accomplished waiting 6 months to get my house sold, and actually sold it for less than I could had I priced it properly in the beginning because by the time I had an offer on it the market in that town had slowed and the weather had turned very wintery.

———

———

Realist Estimates

———

Licensed realtors typically have a tool called "realist" or an equivalent system which is available through their MLS.

———

Realist estimates are generated in a similar way to Zillow Zestimates with the exception the the realtor can add and eliminate comparable homes to improve accuracy, as well as the fact that the sale pries are actually data from sales and NOT estimates like Zillow uses.

———

This results in value ranges that are quick to give a reasonably accurate price range for a home. The key thing being that it's combining an automated process with an experienced licensed realtor to arrive at a quick estimate. This is a good tool that realtors use to "ballpark" but it is not a substitute for a CMA or Comparative market analysis.

———

This tool will often be used by buyer's agents that have not done a full CMA when guiding their clients in putting together an offer and will often become very important to the perceived market value of the home.

———

What is a CMA - Comparative Market Analysis?

WHAT IS A CMA

When speaking to a realtor you'll often hear the acronym CMA referring to a Comparative Market Analysis. This is an examination of current market conditions, recent comparable sales, current homes on the market (the competition) and the realtor's experience and knowledge compiled into a detailed report.

———

Realtors typically prepare a CMA when assisting a seller in pricing their home so that it will sell in a reasonable amount of time for a fair price. CMA's can be basic, or highly detailed depending on the complexity of the estimate. Some factors that a realtor will typically take into account are:

———

Recent sales
- Location
- Style

- Distressed vs Non distressed sale
- Similar quality / condition / finishes etc...

———

CMA's can be done quickly or can be very useful and depending on the situation may be done quickly or tailored to the client's needs. They will typically be a good estimation of market and lending value but are NOT a substitute for a full appraisal by a licensed appraiser.

———

What is an Appraisal?

WHAT IS AN APPRAISAL

When speaking to a realtor, to the bank, etc... you'll often hear them talking about an appraisal. An appraisal is similar to a CMA but it is typically more detailed, more through, and is performed by a licensed appraiser - someone who makes their entire living based on accurately assessing the market value of real estate. Appraisers are typically hired by the lender in a transaction in order to protect the lender by giving a completely independent opinion on the market value of a property.

For an explanation of what the different types of appraisals are, and how they are used in specific situations I recommend the following article:

https://en.wikipedia.org/wiki/Real_estate_appraisal

We have already discussed much of what goes into determining a home's marketable value, and I just don't want to bore you too much with extra details that you may not need.

————

What does it mean if a realtor, an appraiser, buyer, or bank tells you a home has been over improved?

————

Over Improved is the term you'll hear when you see that $100,000 market value home with a $50,000 deck, $20,000 in landscaping, marble floors, high end fixtures, and the best of everything throughout. The owner may have added $90,000 in upgrades to a home that the top comparable in the area sold for $100,000. His home is only worth $100,000 not the $190,000 because the improvements. This initially doesn't make sense to people because logic would initially dictate that if I bought a $100,000 home and added $90,000 worth of improvements, that the home would now be worth $190,000. This is the biggest problem that most people have in accurately understanding the market value of their own home. The pride of ownership, and appreciation for the things that have been added are very personal to the seller, and were added for the seller's enjoyment and are typically not considered in determining market value.

————

Even if the buyer appreciates the improvements the bank will not lend based on a value that is greater than the comparable sales in the neighborhood without an exceptionally good reason. So that house even after all of the improvements is still worth only $100,000 to a bank, and consequently $100,000 to a buyer because that's how much they can borrow to purchase it.

———

A couple of examples I was showing a home that comps were supporting a $300,000 loanable value to a buyer. The seller was asking $390,000 initially because of the upgrades he had made to the home. He had a 3 level Trex deck, that he had spent roughly $100,000 building along with the patio and boardwalk in the back yard. His landscaping had cost him over $50,000 to put in and roughly $10,000 year to maintain. And it was absolutely beautiful in every way, the yard could have been featured in a landscaping magazine. From the buyer's perspective, they loved the large beautiful deck, and loved looking at the landscaping, but were concerned about the cost of maintaining the landscaping. In the buyers mind, the deck was a bonus, and had some added value but the landscaping actually DECREASED the perceived value to the buyer. This home eventually sold after a year and a half on the market for significantly less than $300,000. The seller ended up settling for over $100,000 less than the original listing price.

———

I suspect that the landscaping was the biggest factor to many potential buyers. The point I am making is that even with over $100,000 in ADDED improvements to an immaculate home in a desirable neighborhood, the home sat on the market for over a year and sold BELOW the market average. Why? The top end of the homes value was determined by what a bank would lend, and then buyers deducted for what they thought the burden of maintaining or removing the landscaping would be worth to them.

———

Does this mean that you shouldn't improve your home? Absolutely not! The seller loved his home and lived happily in it for many years, enjoyed the landscaping, enjoyed the deck, raised children to adulthood, and had a lot of great memories. But when you do something that improves a home over and above market value you are investing in your personal enjoyment not in the value of your home.

———

My personal advice? Maintain your home well, fix things that break quickly, make modest improvements like remodeling an out of date kitchen or updating painting and carpets. These things both enhance your personal enjoyment and MAINTAIN your homes market value. However, if you have a $300,000 home and you're thinking of spending $100,000 in upgrades that will not make your home worth $400,000 do yourself a favor, sell your $300,000 home and buy yourself a $400,000 home, you'll get what you wanted, and your money will be safer.

Chapter Four

PRICING

We have looked at how home values are determined, how each party in the sale views them, and why. Next we will look at pricing your home vs the market in order to get the best sale price AND a fast sale.

———

Basically when pricing your home for sale we have four basic options:

———

- Pricing above market value = few showings + fewer offers & long time on market
- Price at Market Value = adequate showings & offers
- Price lower than market value = Many showings + often multiple offers = fast sale at good price
- Auction situations = multiple offers unpredictable final value because of time constraints. Can sell

high or low without much control or predictability.

————

Looking at each of these in more detail we will find that each has a situation where it makes sense but as a seller it's important to understand the impact that each of these strategies will have on the time your home is on the market as well as its eventual selling price.

————

Pricing a home above market value seems to make sense initially to most sellers and is the mistake that the vast majority of unsuccessful sellers that have done an otherwise good job of preparing their home for sale have made. Sellers and inexperienced agents often insist on pricing a home above market value. And at first this seems to make sense, you can always lower your price, right? And why should I leave money on the table? I don't want to get less than my home is worth. I put so much into it that it's worth more than the other houses on the market and the buyers will appreciate that when they see it... are a few of the things that most buyers say when deciding to follow this strategy.

————

In practice, when a home is priced above market value it generates fewer showings by potential buyers because they will view the home as equivalent to similar size and configuration homes that are currently on the market. If a home is the same square footage, number of bedrooms, bathrooms, etc... as 30 other similar homes on the market and it is priced 10%,

20% or 30% higher it will generate less interest from serious qualified buyers. Fewer inquiries, = fewer showings = fewer offers. And if it does get an offer, expect the offer to be at market value, and if you get lucky and get an offer at full asking price, there is a very good chance that the bank will refuse to finance it once the appraiser says that the home is worth significantly less. You are left in this situation with the only option being a buyer that is paying cash, or has enough cash to cover the difference between the loan value and the offer amount. For example if you are selling a home for a contracted price of $100,000 and the appraiser assigns a value of $80,000 then the buyer will have to pay an extra $20,000 out of their own pocket in order for the bank to agree to make the loan. I have seen this happen, but it is extremely rare to find this unicorn buyer that not only WANTS your home so much they are willing to overpay, but has the resources to make it work when the bank won't lend the full amount.

———

More often when a home has been priced above the market value the interested qualified buyers have viewed the home and moved on to other options, and when the seller finally lowers the price to market value after a few months or years on the market buyers have the feeling that there is something wrong with the house, and will still avoid it. The most common end result from pricing a home above market value is a home that sits on the market for a long time, scares away buyers, and eventually sells below market value.

———

Pricing at market value based on recent comparable sales and your homes condition is the most often recommended strategy by most realtors and for good reason. Pricing at market value yields a good amount of showings with a high likelihood of fair market value offers in a short amount of time. In a slow real estate market with excess inventory compared to the number of buyers this strategy works. In a fast market with many more buyers than homes on the market, this strategy still works, and this is why it's the most often recommended strategy by realtors.

———

Pricing below market value is a strategy that most home-owners are unwilling to try but many investors, banks and flippers use regularly in order to sell a home as fast as possible for as much as possible. Why would you ever want to set an asking price for less than market value? Two words: Multiple Bids! Pricing a home 10%, 20% or more lower than market value seems like it would drive the selling price down. However in practice it tends to drive the price up to and sometimes above market value bu creating competition.

———

Why does it work this way? Consider the housing market in your town.... If there are 30 similar 3 bed 2 bath homes of similar size and neighborhood that fit buyer's needs on the market and there are 30 buyers in the market. This is a balanced market - if all 30 homes were priced exactly alike and were in the exact same condition they would all expect to get exactly one bid at full asking price and all buyers and sellers would be satisfied. However if 20 of the homes are priced at market value, 5 above market value and 5 below market value - the 5 below market value will get the attention of all 30 buyers who would like to get a good deal. So now you have 5 below market houses that have 30 buyers competing for them. The 20 that are priced at market value will likely get offers only after the 5 less expensive equivalent houses have sold, and the 5 over market value are not getting offers because there are less expensive options and they are only serving to increase competition for the below market and at market value homes.

––––––

So lets expand this example.

1. 30 buyers in the market for a $200,000 4 bedroom house in your town USA

2. There are 30 equivalent $200,000 market value 4 bedroom homes homes for sale = perfectly balanced market.

3. 5 are priced below market - if all 30 buyers bid evenly that is 6 bidders home (5 houses / 30 bidders = 6 bids) - and buyers will typically go for the supply of lower cost options before bidding on the remaining inventory. However what we actually see in real life is something more like this in 45 days on market:

4. House A - $150,000 - 20 offers / house sells for $205,000

5. House B&C - $175,000 - 10 offers / Sells for $203,000

6. House D - $185,000 - 6 offers / Sells for $208,000

7. House E - $195,000 - 4 offers Sells for $201,000

8. 20 houses are prices at Market Value - $200,000

9. These houses will have many showings and each

will expect 1-3 market value offers $195,000 - $200,000
10. 5 houses are priced over Market Value
11. House F - $210,000 - 1 market value offer @ $200,000
12. Houses G&H - $220,000 - 0 offers stayed on market 6 months longer than competition
13. House I - $230,000 - 0 offers stayed on market 8 months longer than competition before selling at market value
14. House J - $250,000 - 0 offers stayed on market 18 months longer than competition before selling at market value

———

The houses that were priced below market generated significantly more interest and had the majority of the buyers in the market viewed and put bids on one or more of the homes. This created a sense of urgency and competition that resulted in multiple bids and serious buyers bidding over market value to make sure they "won".

———

The homes that were at market value generally all sold only once the previous inventory was exhausted and the above market value homes were largely ignored except for the one that was priced only slightly above market got an actual market value offer yet still sold for less than many homes that were priced lower because there was no competition or urgency for this home. And I know you've been doing the math, and are saying, "But John, there's still 4 more buyers left, won't they have to buy the overpriced homes now?".

Well, not exactly. While 26 of these homes sold another 26 came on the market, along with another 26 buyers keeping the inventory and buyers in balance and the dynamics ongoing over time. And while there are swings to buyer's markets when there's more inventory than buyers, and price trends lower, and seller's markets when there's more buyers than inventory and prices trend higher, the overall dynamic within that market stays the same. Homes that are priced at or below market sell, and homes that are priced higher help the homes that are priced fairly sell by creating a perception of greater value for those homes.

————

Auctions are another way that people get value from homes while selling quickly. The advantage to an auction is that as a seller you are letting the market determine the value in a definite time and place. It also fosters competition and the chance of getting greater value than traditional marketing. However it does have the downside of unpredictability. Auctions work well for an in demand property, in a seller's market. In a balanced market, or a buyer's market auctions are still a great way to quickly liquidate but are high risk as far as getting full value goes.

CALCULATING NET PROCEEDS

Another consideration in determining how much you can sell your home for is knowing what your net proceeds will be after a sale. This is more complicated than simply taking the selling price - what you owe on your mortgage.

In a perfect world it would be easy
    $200,000 Sale Price
    $100,000 Mortgage Balance

    $100,000 Net proceeds from sale

Unfortunately the world is not perfect and we have other things to consider such as realtor fees, taxes, closing costs, title company, point of sale fees and more.

———

A really simple way to get an idea is to Google- "Real Estate Net Proceeds Calculator" - there are also many apps available on the iPhone app store and Google Play.

———

A few things that you'll expect to include will be:

- Sale Price of the Home
- Real Estate Commission
- Balance of First Mortgage
- Balance of Other Liens
- Property Taxes
- Seller's Portion of Closing Costs
- Seller Concessions for FHA or VA loans

———

This means that for the $200,000 selling price above with a $100,000 balance on your Mortgage you may only net $80,000 after all of the other costs have been accounted for.

———

Knowing your expected net is important to know BEFORE you list your home so you'll know the minimum you can accept for an offer and any other costs and concessions for selling your home. There's nothing worse than getting to the closing table and being surprised by the amount you have left over after selling.

Chapter Five

FSBO VS HIRING A REALTOR

The great debate most home sellers have with themselves is whether to market their home as a for sale by owner (FSBO) or list it with a Realtor.

———

Full disclosure, I am obviously a Realtor, and I know how to market a home better than the average homeowner because marketing homes successfully is how I feed my family. That being said I am not against homeowners marketing their homes FSBO, I have bought and sold FSBO when I have known the buyer or seller, and have even advised close friends market their homes as FSBO when the math just wouldn't work for them to pay a real estate fee. Again, my ethical and moral responsibility is to help people first, not make money off of people. I will personally make more money by doing good in the world and helping people without regard to my own self interest than I ever will by taking advantage of someone. Many realtors will try to use scare tactics to convince homeowners to list with them instead of selling their home as an FSBO. This goes against my moral compass, and I won't do that here, instead I will give you advice on how to do it successfully. * Remember I am not an attorney - nothing below constitutes legal advice please consult your attorney with specific questions regarding liability.

If you are considering selling your home yourself there are several things you need to do.

1. Find out what the accurate market value supported by recent comparable sales is for your home and price it accordingly. (An ethical realtor should be willing to help you get an estimate even if you don't list with them - if you have a hard time finding one, I will be glad to help you)
2. Follow the earlier steps in the book about preparing your home for sale - this is equally important if you FSBO or list with a realtor.
3. Have professional photographs made of your home - the simple truth is that quality photographs, properly edited, framed, lit, and retouched can have a significant impact on the number of showings, offers, and selling price of your home.
4. Make sure your home is advertised in as many places online as possible. Spend money on postcard marketing campaigns, newspaper ads online marketing on google, facebook etc... to publicize your home for sale to generate buyer traffic.
5. Advertise and hold open houses & consider a broker's open to introduce yourself to as many buyer's agents as possible and get their unbiased

feedback on how to better market your home yourself. (Reputable ethical realtors should be willing to give you this feedback without being pushy in trying to get you to list with them. Most realtors are actually very easy to get along with just be professional with them and they will be with you in return)

6. Be willing to work with buyer's agents - typically buyer's agents will expect 2.5%-3% of the selling price for selling your home even if it's an FSBO. Right in your ads mention that you're willing to work with buyer's agents and pay a fee. Most agents will steer their buyers to sellers that are easy to work with, and only if they can get paid for doing their job.

7. Remember that in an FSBO situation the buyer's agent represents the BUYER not you. They still have a legal and ethical responsibility to treat you fairly, but they do NOT owe you confidentiality. Anything you tell them they have a legal obligation to tell their buyers.

8. Selling FSBO does NOT remove your obligation to disclose defects in the home visible or hidden.

9. Selling FSBO also DOES keep much of the liability for anything that goes wrong with the sale of the home with the seller. Anything misrepresented to a buyer even accidentally, paperwork messed up, etc... will be on you without a realtor representing your interests or sharing that liability with you.

10. DO hire an experienced real estate attorney to review offers that come in and help you in the sale process. Purchase agreements can be potentially heavily slanted in favor of one party or another and

without someone experienced representing you it opens you up to being taken advantage of in the process.

———

Cost

Obviously most people decide to do the FSBO route because they would like to save money. And this is a very valid reason. In reality though to do a quality job marketing your home and protecting yourself legally it will still cost you money, particularly if a buyer's agent is involved (And unfortunately for those of us that have marketed homes FSBO almost all buyers will utilize the service of an agent when they purchase)

———

So on a $200K home FSBO selling cost you should expect:

- $400 - Cost to list home in MLS as FSBO
- $6,000 - Buyer's Agent Fee
- $2,500 - Attorney to draft & review purchase agreements
- $500 - Photographer
- $1,500 - $2,500 - Misc total / printing costs for classified ads, yard signs, postcards, info sheets, cost of open house / advertising etc....

———

Total typical cost to sell as FSBO $10,900-$11,900
Total cost to advertise FSBO if it does NOT sell - Approximately $2,000-$3,000

Cost to hire a realtor to market and advertise the home $0 pay $10,000-$12,000 commission ONLY if it sells.

————

But John, my neighbor, father, uncle.... Etc... sold a home FSBO and he didn't pay a buyer's agent, priced the house himself, skipped the attorney, and never put out an ad or an open house. He saved all that money that a greedy realtor would take from him. When I hear this I say GREAT!!! One of two things happened, they got lucky and found a buyer without advertising who paid fair market value without needing a realtor or attorney. OR they underpriced their home so low that the first person that heard about it came along and took advantage of them because they didn't know the market value of their property. I have done the same thing. I've sold property FSBO to the next door neighbor with not attorneys, realtors, or anything involved. But I also knew the fair market value with a high degree of certainty, and had a buyer that I didn't have to spend money marketing to in order to find. If you have a situation like that, there's no reason to hire a realtor. Don't waste your money, I wouldn't waste my own. But if you have to market the property to find a buyer, a realtor assumes all of the marketing cost, much of the liability, and does the work of dealing with the contracts, closing process, represents your interests against the buyers, and generally insulates you from all of the mind numbing maddening stuff that goes on between offer and closing. Additionally because a professional realtor does this for a living, they are pretty good at it and aren't caught by surprise by the unexpected things that go wrong during the process.

WHAT TO EXPECT WITH A REALTOR

———

What should you expect when marketing your home with a realtor?

———

A qualified realtor should be able to explain the steps that they will take to help you sell your home. As with anything not all realtors are exactly the same, and you can't expect the same results from one that you would get with another. Some realtors are part time hobbyists, some are high volume power agents. Some are low volume high service, some specialize in high end luxury homes, while others specialize in low end inexpensive houses. And others specialize in a specific community or neighborhood.

———

As you can see each of these realtors is likely to take a

different approach to marketing your home and that's not a bad thing. The important thing is to hire a realtor that will fit your needs and who understands and will develop a quality marketing plan and follow through with that for your type of home, in your location at the time you are selling. Personally I turn away listings even from family and friends if they are in a market that I'm unfamiliar with, or I just feel I won't be successful with. I'll gladly research the agents that do a good job in that market and provide a personal referral to make sure that they get the best realtor for their specific needs. I specialize in higher value homes in the Greater Cleveland and Akron Ohio Markets (NorthEast Ohio) because I can provide high touch personal service to my clients. I'm not a high volume sell 300 houses a year with my face on a billboard kind of realtor. There is nothing wrong with that kind of realtor, but I just enjoy being able to take the time to get to know my clients personally, and provide the kind of service to them that makes a friend for life, not just a customer. I mean I'm working with you on the most important life changing decision you'll likely make in the near future.... That's a time for personal service, not high volume. I also usually to work with higher value homes priced between $250,000 in my Home Area of Hudson, Twinsburg, Solon, Aurora, Macedonia Ohio and surrounding communities and luxury properties worth up to millions of dollars throughout NorthEast Ohio. This allows me to be aggressive and still give the warm personal attention that my clients deserve.

———

You'll notice that most of what I set out for you to do to market your home are the same things that I would expect a realtor to be doing to market your home. The difference is that instead of you paying several thousand dollars and assuming all of the risk of your home not selling the realtor is paying advertising, gas, photographers mailing flyers and postcards, going door to door in neighborhoods to let people know that the home is on the market, etc... The bottom line is that a professional realtor should be aggressively taking steps to get attention for your home in order to make it sell at market price in the shortest time possible. All at no cost or risk to the seller unless the home successfully sells.

————

What should you expect your realtor to do to market your home?

————

1. **Tell you the accurate market value supported by recent comparable sales** is for your home and advise you to price it accordingly.
2. **Consult with you on preparing your home for sale** including items that need fixed, decluttering, etc...
3. **Have professional photographs made of your home** - the simple truth is that quality photographs, properly edited, framed, lit, and retouched can have a significant impact on the number of showings, offers, and selling price of your home. DO NOT UNDER ANY CIRCUMSTANCE HIRE A REALTOR WHO USES A CELL PHONE OR POINT AND SHOOT TO TAKE PHOTOS OF YOUR $100K + HOME they are costing you showings, offers, and time which means you'll either not sell or sell below market.

4. **Make sure your home is advertised in as many places online as possible.** A good realtor should not just push to the MLS and wait to see what happens. They should be aggressively marketing your home on other classified sites, social media, etc...

5. **Advertise and hold open houses & consider a broker's open** - Many homes sell just fine without either of these steps being taken. But if you have a home that is properly priced, properly marketed, and has an aggressively marketed open house early in its sales cycle it will generate buyer traffic and feedback and many times the appearance of competition for the home resulting in a faster sale at a stronger price.

6. **Be unselfish to pay buyer's agents** - typically buyer's agents will expect 2.5%-3% of the selling price for selling your home many listing agents aggressively discount the buyer's agent side of the transaction even down to 1-2% to cover their own costs in marketing the home. I have always believed in paying higher fees to buyer's agents even if it lowers my own income. Buyer's agents are human, and could be expected to be more enthusiastic towards a home with a better payout.

7. **Represent you and your best interests** during the course of the marketing, the negotiation, closing and after closing. Realtor's job is to have your best interests in mind, and have your back at all times.

WHAT DOES A REALTOR COST

What does a realtor cost and why?

———

A realtor typically works on a commission only basis and there is no "Standard" fee that a realtor charges. Each broker-age, and realtor may have guidelines that they work with, and different markets throughout the country have varying commission structures that are common within the market.

———

I can only speak to my own market of Northeast Ohio. Here common residential commissions range from a flat 7% to tiered commissions that decline as the price of the house goes higher.

———

For example a typical declining graduated fee structure may look like:

7% first $100K
6% to $200K
5% to 300k
4% to 500K
3% over 500K

———

So for a home that sells for $350,000 the commission would typically be calculated as follows:

———

$7,000 - 7% first $100K
$6,000 - 6% to $200K
$5,000 - 5% to $300K
$2,000 - 4% of 50K

_____

$20,000 - Total

———

A flat rate of 7% would look like:

$350,000 X .07 = $24,500
$350,000 X .06 = $21,000
$350,000 X .05 = $17,500

The first reaction from sellers tends to be - I want to get my real estate license because that's more $ than I made last Week / month / year/ decade etc... And yes there is a sticker shock when you first look at the numbers but remember that the realtor doesn't get paid all of that money, there are several people usually involved in a transaction who each get paid.

———

- Listing Agent
- Listing Brokerage
- Selling Agent
- Selling Broker

———

Each side typically gets roughly 50% of the fee so for example a $20,000 commission goes $10,000 to buyer's agent / brokerage and $10,000 to the listing agent and brokerage. Typical splits between an agent and his brokerage can range between 50-70% that the agent keeps from their commissions. So the listing and selling agent will probably end up with $5K-$7K for doing months worth of work, putting many miles on their cars, paying monthly feel to their brokerage, liability insurance, health insurance, realtor board dues, continuing education, office, phones, software, etc...

———

Additionally the listing agent if they have done their job properly has spent significant money on advertising, postage, photography etc... to market your home, many times this cost runs into several thousand dollars per home, especially on higher end homes and their net per home for doing months worth of work and taking on significant liability is very low.

———

it's not unusual for an agent to have costs of $1K-$2K per month in overhead whether they sell a home or not.

———

The average part time agent is spending $8K a year to make less than $12K in net commissions. They are not in the business to get rich quick, they are in it to help people. In other words you cannot feed a family by selling a couple of homes per year, and agents that are in an area that sell $100K homes are going to be grossing about $1,000 - $1500 per sale. This is a hard work business that rewards very few realtors, which is why as a seller you have so many desperate realtors harassing you, and cutting their fees to the bone to entice you with their low fees while not being able to afford to do the marketing needed to sell your home quickly at market value.

TYPES OF REALTORS

―――

Spotting the high volume low personal service agent - This agent can be spotted by perusing your local supermarket or local community paper. They have a bad photograph and a cheesy tagline that repeats the words sell, sold, sale, etc... around their name. They desperately want you to know that they sell homes for sale until they are sold. They'll tell you that nobody sells more homes than they do and nobody has more homes for sale right now than them, and nobody charges less. Their pitch is not about service or quality but about being cheap and fast.

―――

A typical high volume low service agents ad will look like:
   Joe Smith is a house SOLD name
   Sally Smith is about to set SALE

———

There's nothing wrong with being a high volume low service agent. These agents are good at what they do which is working with a lot of people as quickly as possible and charging low fees to do it. They are the wall-mart of the industry and serve a valuable place within it.

———

High Service Low Volume Agent - This agent specializes within a market segment sometimes by geography, neighborhood, type of home or real estate. They may work only with investors, only work in their hometown, only work in a specific price range etc... this agent usually has a highly engaged highly targeted list of contacts within the industry as well as potential buyers for your home. They may have less name recognition in the overall market, but within their niche they are the most knowledgable, well connected, and effective agents. They typically spend more time, effort, and money to market each home and typically result in higher offers in less time for their sellers.

———

Team Leaders - This agent while similar to the high volume low service agent can be spotted by the fact that their name is on every sign in town yet none of their clients have ever met them. In their place they have several team members that meet buyers and sellers and handle a lot of the transactions for them. While the team is doing volume overall, the coach is working behind the scenes to make the team strong, calling the plays and providing opportunities for the team members. Teams can be high touch low volume, or low touch high volume, and just like the individual agents each agent within a team may have different focus and niche than the rest.

———

OK then John what kind of agent are you? - If you're in my niche market, lets get together and you can find out and decide for yourself. While I do have a team - "Your Neighborhood Experts" at Platinum Real Estate which has as of the date of this writing in December 2017 sold 443 homes in the last 12 months between Northeast Ohio and Naples and Miami Fl earning a 5/5 star rating on Zillow with 87 reviews along the way. I work primarily in higher end markets with high service and low volume while the strength of having a 39 member team helps market homes more effectively for my clients. This means that any home that I market is aggressively marketed in all media, print, direct mail, open houses, online, social media, and face to face. When I take on a client I start out with the attitude that someday we are going to run into each other at Walmart, or a restaurant or wherever. And I truly want that to be a happy reunion. That can only happen if I have treated you with the same care and respect that I would my own family.

MARKETING STRATEGIES

———

Real estate marketing is a largely visual medium in the age of online MLS and social media.

———

In a statistic that I am making up on the spot - literally every homebuyer looks online first. Much like internet dating has changed the landscape of how we meet our partners, and auto trader has changed how we shop for cars, home buyers look online first the vast majority of the time. Websites like Realtor.com, Zillow, Trulia, Facebook, Craigslist, etc... have replaced the Sunday paper as the primary information source that home buyers use.

———

What is the first thing a buyer judges your home on in our swipe right swipe left culture? That's right it's the photograph. A bad primary photo won't get a click to check out the rest of the house. And bad pictures - pictures that are too dark, taken with a cell phone, taken at bad angles, badly touched up etc... kill off buyer demand faster than Scooby and the gang finding a bucket of glow in the dark paint in the basement.

––––––

And if someone comes to see your house in person, when they leave and go home to think about which home to put an offer in on, what are they going to do? Yep, they're going back online and checking out the photos. The photos that you or your realtor place in the MLS are not only the first impression that buyers get, but also the lasting impression the will have because in another entirely made up statistic every buyer ever goes back to the online listing an average of 999,002 times to look at the photos again and again before making their decision. Your photos simply HAVE to make a good impression if you want to get a quick full value sale.

––––––

Tips for photographing your home regardless of whether you FSBO or use a Realtor

- When selling your home demand high quality well lit photos taken with a quality DSLR NOT a cell phone.
- The photographer should have extra lighting, umbrellas, flashes, led's to light up dark areas of the rooms.
- The DSLR will probably be set up on a tripod to take more stable pictures.

- Use of a circular polarized filter on exterior shots with a high quality portrait lens (50mm) tends to make the home look big and the sky bright.
- Interior shots should be done with a wide angle NOT fish eye lens and have the lens distortion, and color corrected in software such as Adobe Lightroom prior to posting online
- You have the right to ask your agent about this PRIOR to listing the home with them.

I am not a fan of some of the over processed photos that are common nowadays. Some people overprices the photos to the point that they look cartoonish and fake. I have seen the best results with quality shots, that make a room appear bright, open and free of clutter. I like the house to look colorful yet natural. And I do most of my own photography - I'll typically spend several hours photographing a house and several more in post production. When appropriate I'll hire a full time professional photographer, but only ones that meet my standards and have a proven track record of real estate photography.

Chapter Six

PREPARING FOR SHOWINGS

You've done your CMA's have your house priced right, advertising is done right, and your photos look amazing. Now you are about to get the phone call that someone wants to come see your house!!!! At first you're excited, then in a panic you look around and realize that you are ready because you followed the advice in the preparing your home for sale chapter. No longer panicking, you look yourself in the mirror and whisper, "You Got This"!

———

One of the most stressful parts of selling a home is showings. There are fewer things that are less natural than having strangers in your home when you aren't there, touring every room, and judging everything about your home from it's decor, it's cleanliness, the back yard, the drapes, the floors..... And ..... And..... Ok.... Breathe.......

———

If you are using a realtor your home will be shown only when a licensed realtor is with the buyers. You have the right to require pre-qualified buyers only, have the right to be present if you'd like, or just do the traditional thing and find something to do for an hour and trust the system that works.

———

If you are worried about your personal belongings, theft, snooping, etc... first make sure your valuables, jewelry, etc... are in storage, in a safe, or somehow removed from areas where sticky fingers could find them. A second recommendation is to purchase an inexpensive security cam or nanny cam an leave it in the rooms you are concerned with. Very inexpensive plug and play systems are available starting at $25 for a "Stuart Cam" that looks like a minion (from the animated movie Despicable Me) at Walmart. I use these and not only do they look cute, but they can be motion sensitive and support two way audio. The best part is there's no monthly fee and you can watch in real time what's happening on your cell phone from anywhere in the world that you have data or wifi.

———

Have a plan for your pets one of the most common things as a realtor is walking into a home that has pets and not knowing where they are. Many buyers and realtors are bitten by dogs every year, pets escape to run neighborhoods, and literally anything can go wrong. If you have pets, please develop a plan for them for during showings. If you can take them with you in carriers, that is a great solution. If you are able to confine them to a kennel also a great solution. I know not everyone like doing that but locking them in a laundry room is common. The downside? Buyers even if they've been told not to are going to want to peek into the laundry room and now fido and fluffy are probably not staying put. If the pets have to stay, please communicate with the agent, the showing service, and most of all hang a sign on the door that says the pet is in there, and what kind it is. This keeps everyone including your pet safer.

———

Sometimes showings don't happen exactly as planned. If a showing is supposed to happen between 1-1:30 have a plan that gives you till 2:00. Seriously, take your time, relax and enjoy it. Maybe even schedule a couple of houses to look at yourself at that time. Buyers that are serious tend to stay longer and that's a good sign. Make the best of this and enjoy it!

———

My golden rule is keep your home 20 minutes away from showing condition at all times.

If you have kids and pets, this is NOT easy. I try this in my own home and as a single father raising two kids by myself I can tell you my home is not always showing ready even in 4 hours of cleaning. So I get it, what I will say is when your home is for sale it's a team effort. Dishes can be stashed in the dishwasher if you don't have time to wash them, if you have a storage space unit use it for anything you don't want lying around. Brown boxes can be stacked in the basement or garage in order to hide last minute clutter.

———

Be creative, and most of all keep the house smelling fresh. Air fresheners and glade plugins can go a long way. Don't overdo it though, it's important not to look like you're overcompensating.

Tips

- Keep small trash bags handy in high traffic rooms of the house where junk tends to collect
- Having a storage area for panic cleaning and utilizing cardboard or plastic containers to stack in garages or basement corners can cut down on time
- Decluttering and removing items that are not often used will cut down on the number of messes made significantly
- Clean things that tend to show dirt like bathtubs and toilets daily. They are easy to forget when under pressure, and only take a minute to wipe down if they aren't dirty.
- Eat from paper or plastic dishes for a while - I know it's not environmentally friendly, but if you have trouble keeping up with dirty dishes, this can be a short term solution - just please recycle when you're done
- Most of all have an exit strategy with a checklist that everyone in the house has a job to do, a bathroom to clean a room to vacuum. The more people actively helping, the faster you can be ready for a showing.

Chapter Seven

GETTING OFFERS & NEGOTIATING

You're now sitting in your kitchen killing time on your iPad when the call comes in from your realtor. You have an offer coming on your house. Suddenly the emotions overlap, excitement, sadness, happiness, nervousness you don't know what to expect and you just ask….. "How much"

Getting an offer on your house is the goal of all of the preparation and marketing we've done up to this point. Now you have an offer and its time to find out what the buying public thinks your house is worth. Y**our realtor says, "We have a strong offer I'll send it to you by e-mail to review."**

———

The offer will come to you by whatever means you have discussed with your realtor. Some customers want everything in person, others want things faxed, others use digital signatures like a pro. The key is to get the offer in the way that you are comfortable with, and by all means READ the entire offer and ask your realtor questions about it. They can explain the basic provisions of the purchase agreement and what it means but they cannot give you legal advice. If you have an attorney you have the right to have the attorney review it. (I personally use and like legalshield - and no I'm not pushing it on you and I don't belong to their affiliate or reseller plan, I just use the service for reviewing documents that I want a basic legal opinion on - they will review documents for free and you get a licensed attorney's opinion and explanation).

———

The offer will contain various sections

1. The offer - this will include things like the amount of the offer and earnest money
2. The contingencies - timeframe for inspections, and remedies if there are any - additional provisions for contingencies such as contingent on financing, house sale, etc... can be there
3. The timeframe
4. The title company - the title company is always specified in the purchase agreement. You can accept this or request your own be used if you have a favorite.
5. The agents involved - the listing and selling agents and their respective brokers will be listed
6. Signature area - all involved parties will sign
7. Any addendum - as with any contract it may have additional conditions that are not specified in the original boilerplate agreement. They will usually be attached at the end.

8. An agency disclosure - this is a separate paper that lists the agents, and their roles as well as the respective brokers and their roles in relation to the buyer and seller to specify acknowledgment from all parties as to who is being represented by whom.
9. Proof of funds / ability to purchase - in a cash sale, this may be a bank statement, a letter from the bank, or in a financing it will be a letter from a bank saying that the buyer is qualified.

———

It is slightly more complicated than this but you'll be able to follow the paperwork and just knowing what is coming is the important part.

———

Once you have read your offer, you have a few options.

———

1. Accept the offer as-is
2. Reject the offer
3. Counter offer
4. Do nothing and hold the offer

———

These are pretty self explanatory, but accepting the offer is simply saying, yes, I am happy with the offer in it's present state, signing it and sending it back to the buyer. As soon as you have done that you are under contract and we are working towards closing.

―――――

Rejecting the offer is done when it's just not even close and you don't want to counter for any reason. You can give an explanation, or just reject it silently by saying no. Once you reply to the buyer that you are rejecting the offer they can submit a new offer, or choose to move on.

―――――

Counter-offering happens when you get an offer that you do not wish to accept and you propose new terms that you would accept. For example your asking price is $300K, they offered you $290K and you counter offer $295K.

A few things to know about counter offers

- An original offer is the first half of a contract.
- If you accept it you have a valid contract
- If you reject it there is no contract both parties are free
- If you counter offer - the ORIGINAL offer is gone and cannot be accepted your counter offer is binding if the buyer signs.
- Only counter if you are willing to lose the original offer.

―――――

Finally you can do nothing and hold the offer for as long as the offer is valid. Many offers are valid for a set time, 24 hours, 1 week, 1 month etc... You can hold the offer and choose to accept it any time prior to it expiring and you have a contract. UNLESS the seller revokes the offer before you accept it. Holding offers is often done when there are multiple offers coming in and the seller wants to accept the highest and best offer. The risk is you can lose an offer by holding it too long if the buyer is still looking at other properties.

————

————

How do you know if an offer is strong or weak?

If you have multiple offers sometimes it is a good idea to weigh all of them prior to choosing.

————

Some offers are stronger than others - meaning less likely to fall through

Stronger offers:

- All cash
- Conventional financing with more than enough cash available to cover LTV
- Pre-approval on both the buyer's credit AND the home you are selling.
- Fewer contingencies for things like inspections and financing
- Shorter close time

————

Weaker offers

- Low / No money down
- Require seller concessions or owner financing
- Require sale of previous residence
- Pre-qualification NOT pre-approval
- Many inspections and contingencies that allow the buyer to back out of the deal during contract period

From a seller's point of view, you want the strongest offer you can get, strong buyer with few contingencies. From a buyer's point of view they want options to back out if something goes wrong.

———

The solution is to have fair contingencies. Contingencies for financing, and inspection are very standard and should be expected in the majority of real estate deals. Timelines and remedy periods should be an appropriate amount of time to keep the deal moving forward while allowing due diligence to be performed.

Chapter Eight

THE CLOSING PROCESS

There are several people you will deal with in the contract period / closing process.

———

- The Inspectors
- The Appraiser
- The Title Agency
- The Mortgage Lender
- The Listing Agent
- The Buyers Agent
- Attorneys (less frequently)

———

Each of these people has a valuable role during the closing process and are there to protect their respective clients. Generally everyone involved feels a genuine desire to get the deal done for both the buyer and the seller, but complications can and do arise during this stage.

You are now under contract, and your listing in the MLS is now showing "Contingent" Time for inspections.

Common inspections include:

- General Home Inspection
- Septic Inspection
- Point of Sale Inspection
- Wood boring insect Inspection
- Radon inspection
- Mold Inspection
- Asbestos Inspection

Your buyer will elect to have whatever inspection that they need to feel comfortable in their purchase and the process will go something like this....

You will get a phone call letting you know that an inspector is coming to view the house Tuesday at 10am. The inspector may meet you there, or a realtor and they will follow a very thorough checklist that allows them to inspect and document the inspection of electrical, mechanical and structural components of your home. They will look for any obvious and some hidden issues that you may not even have been aware of. They'll climb ladders, crawl into crawlspaces and attics, maybe even put a camera in your sewer pipes.

When they are finished they will issue a report to the buyer.

———

Your agent will call you and forward the inspection report. Now you'll notice that there is a request to fix several items.

- There are bats in your attic because a vent has come loose
- You have a tub drain missing a stopper
- There is no GFCI plug in your bathroom above the sink as required by code.
- There is a 1/4 crack in the concrete near your garage door
- There is a small unnoticed leak in the exhaust for your hot water heater that could be leaking carbon monoxide.

The buyers are now requesting that these items all be fixed in order for them to complete the sale.

———

What are your options?

1. Refuse to fix anything - if the buyers don't agree to buy it now as is the contract is void and you start over. Of course now, you have to disclose the items found on the inspection report and either fix them or face lowball offers, or offers contingent on repairs from the next buyer.
2. Negotiate the list down - You can negotiate with

the buyer - maybe you offer to fix the attic vent, and the GFCI plug and the hot water heater but not the concrete in the garage. If the buyer agrees, you both sign off on it, you perform the repairs OR leave money in escrow for the repairs to be completed after the sale (if the buyer agrees) and you are back under contract and everyone moves forward. If the buyer is saying their list is not negotiable, you have to either accept it or reject it and start over.

3. Agree to fix everything on the list - either perform the repairs to buyers terms (usually proof that a licensed contractor did the repairs) or leave money in escrow to have the repairs performed after the sale if the buyer agrees.

Once the repairs have been made or agreed to be not made, you sign the release of contingencies, and the house goes from "Contingent" to "Pending".

———

———

You are all done with inspections, your home is now showing "Pending" in the MLS letting all fo the other agents know that it's pending financing. What happens next?

———

The next thing you need to be concerned about as a seller is the appraisal. Appraisers are 3rd party independent contractors hired for the bank but not working directly for the bank who give statements of value on real estate for a living. They are very accurate, and very experienced, and highly professional.

––––––––

Much like the inspector, you'll get a call that the appraiser will be out Thursday, at 2PM. Again meet them or a realtor can give them access. The appraiser will take photos, and measurements of your home, and then go back to their office to run comparables. They will make a long elaborate report that if all goes as planned will give a valuation supporting the contract price. Why? Because your agent and the buyer's agent both ran comps and gave good advice and everyone is getting a fair deal at market value.

––––––––

Once the appraiser submits the appraisal report to the bank - the bank will notify the buyer and buyer's agent that the house appraised and that everyone is on track to close.

––––––––

The Title Agency is monitoring the transaction throughout the contract / closing process. They will be in contact with all of the realtors, and the bankers to make sure that when the bank is ready to commit to the loan (Clear to Close) the title search and required filings will all be complete and ready.

––––––––

The title agency will be checking for things like hidden liens, making sure that the mortgages are all released properly, that the money gets from and to the correct people at the right times.

––––––

The main times when you will have contact with them is when you pay your earnest money and when you sign you closing documents. Your realtor and the banker will be in constant contact with them keeping the deal moving forward throughout the process.

––––––

The Banker or Mortgage broker is responsible for guiding the buyer through the steps that they need to go through to get approved for financing, hiring an appraiser to assign a an independent valuation to the property and working with the title agency to make sure that the bank is lending on a property with a clean title.

––––––

The buyer may be required to provide proof of income, residency, assets, etc... in order to satisfy the banks underwriting requirements and to satisfy government regulations. The realtors will be kept in the loop during the process and will be working with the bank and title agency to make sure everything is going smoothly and alert all parties if anything goes wrong.

––––––

The listing agent represents the seller's interest throughout the closing / contract period. They will communicate with the other parties involved in the sale, advise the seller about options they may have, and generally be their "agent" throughout the process keeping communication open ,and protecting the seller from pitfalls that can happen during the closing negotiating solutions to the problems that come up, and recommending experts to assist as needed.

———

The buyer's agent represents the buyer's interest throughout the closing / contract period. They will communicate with the other parties involved in the sale, advise the buyer about options they may have, and generally be their "agent" throughout the process keeping communication open ,and protecting the seller from pitfalls that can happen during the closing negotiating solutions to the problems that come up, and recommending experts to assist as needed.

———

Attorney's are not often involved in residential home sales unless it is a FSBO situation where one party does not have representation. They are more common when buying or selling commercial or investment properties, or when purchasing from a business, estate, or family trust.

Chapter Nine

FINDING YOUR NEW HOME

In today's connected world the first thing most buyers do when searching for a home is go on one of the major real estate search sites like Realtor.com Zillow, Truilia, etc... This is how they find the homes they are interested in, and in many cases, where they find the realtor's they will use during their home search.

————

My parent's generation began their search in the Sunday paper, or at a realtor's office either because they were listed as the listing agent for a home they found in the paper, or because the office was highly visible in a town they were interested in finding a home in. In the days before the inter-net, the only way to get access to the entire inventory of the MLS was through direct contact with a realtor who would have to go into the office and flip through printed books of homes which were updated regularly and shipped to the office. The process meant that the average homebuyer was at the mercy of their realtor because the realtor was literally the gateway to the inventory of homes on the market, and the realtor's knowledge of the local inventory, and their willingness to share it, and their aggressiveness at keeping their clients informed was the key to successfully finding a home. Realtors were considered a partner by a buyer not only because they might be driving a buyer around in a car, but because they were expected to take the time to learn the buyer's wants and needs and actively keep looking until they found the "right fit" for their buyers.

———

In the age of the internet over the last 20 years the tide has slowly shifted to give buyers more control and information. Instead of going to a realtor's office and flipping through paper books or seeing half a dozen choices that your realtor chose to show you, buyers now have the entire MLS at their fingertips online and on their phones. Sites like Realtor.com are updated in almost real time so as a buyer you may know about that great new home that hit the market in the neighborhood you like even before your realtor does. This has lead to the role of a buyer's agent changing, and in many ways the buyer's perception of a buyer's agent has changed however not in the same ways. Buyer's no longer see their agent as the gateway to all home knowledge, but have become very "transactional" with their buyer's agents, viewing them as "door unlockers".

———

Many amateur agents have unfortunately done little to earn the right to be viewed as more than a door unlocked or order taker, but I think it's important to understand what a professional buyer's agent does for their clients.

———

One of the services that I provide my clients is an automatic feed of all new properties available on the MLS as they become available delivered directly to their email.

———

When creating this automatic feed, we take the customer's specific wants and needs for their new property purchase and fine tune a search that meets their expectations. I can create a search list based on criteria such as location, square footage, number of bedrooms, bathrooms, features like basements, garages, etc... The advantage of this over creating similar searches using online tools available to the public is the level of fine grain control that my customer has over exactly which homes they will see in the list.

———

Additionally as new homes come on the market, and higher priced homes have pricing changes that put them in my client's price range they can be notified immediately so that they can request a showing and not miss out on the property they really want.

———

This is a tool that I use myself and that my clients that invest in properties for rentals or fix and flips use regularly because it's the fastest, most accurate and simplest way to ensure that you see every home on the market quickly.

———

When looking at homes you'll often come across a home that has been foreclosed. These homes will typically be owned by a bank, or a government agency such as HUD and marketed through the MLS.

————

There are a few key differences to understand when dealing with a foreclosed home vs. Purchasing from a private seller.

————

When purchasing from a private seller, we are typically negotiating (through realtors) with the owner of the property. This means that there is a single person, couple, or family that has a direct personal interest in the property they are selling. An owner occupant has lived in the home, will have to disclose any issues that the property has they are aware of, and will typically be somewhat efficient to deal with in regard to negotiations of price and terms of the sale. Because the seller has an incentive to sell the home such as relocation, change in life circumstances, or any of the other reasons someone wants to move they will typically be responsive to a buyer's needs to have things like inspections done, repair some reasonable issues that come to light during inspection, and basically act like someone who is genuinely interested in completing the sale in a stress free manner that benefits both parties.

————

The reason many of us are drawn to look at foreclosed homes is usually bang for the buck. Typically foreclosed homes are going to be listed in the MLS for a price that is marginally to significantly below the price that similar homes the the same neighborhood are listed for. As a buyer we need to understand that this does not mean that the home is guaranteed to be a better "value" than a similar home marketed at a higher price. There are several reasons for this:

- Banks often price foreclosed homes below market value to solicit multiple bids
- Banks don't typically offer disclosures on foreclosed homes because they have not lived in them.
- Sales are typically in as is / where is condition - this means that if you find something during inspection, the bank is unlikely to be willing to fix it to complete the sale
- You are often negotiating with a committee instead of a single seller. So motivations to sell may be unclear, and often offers may not get accepted, rejected or countered as quickly as with an owner occupant seller.
- Investors often target foreclosures because they are unconcerned about fixing issues, and they may have an unfair advantage over a casual buyer based on their knowledge of the market, and their ability to self inspect, and self repair issues with the property
- Investors are often making offers with cash and no contingencies, such as inspections, need to sell a current home first, or financing approval. This makes their offers often look "stronger" to a bank because their offer will be much less likely to fall through than the offer of a buyer who is financing to become an owner occupant.

————

Overall these factors among others make purchasing a fore-closed home more difficult and potentially riskier for a buyer looking at a home as a potential owner occupant. That being said, I have bought foreclosed homes in the past including the one I currently live in, and they can be a great value. Some tips for successfully purchasing a foreclosed home are:

- Have your financing in order - Along with your offer you will have to provide proof of funds. A strong financing offer with pre-approvals and a quick close can still stand up against a cash offer for some institutional sellers.
- Take advantage of FHA construction / repair loan programs if they are available for your particular situation.
- Have the property inspected and repairs estimated BEFORE you put in your bid. I know this is hard to do on compressed timelines but it will be needed if you are doing a construction loan vs paying cash.

————

- The bottom line is that buying a foreclosed home can save you money, but it can also cost you more if you run into unforeseen issues with the home. Do your due diligence, be prepared and the process can go smoothly and you can get a great home at below market prices.

————

What does a buyer's agent do?

———

As I mentioned, a buyer's agent is often viewed by buyer's as little more than a "door unlocker". While it's true that agents do unlock doors, they can and do provide significantly more value..... IF you are working with a quality buyer's agent they should do significantly more for you than just open doors. The most common complaints people make about buyer's agents is that they really just don't seem to do anything that adds value to the process. That they schedule showings at homes that the buyer picked out, opened the door, don't know much about the home, and only submit whatever offers the buyer tells them to, can't tell them how much to bid and if it's rejected, ask the buyer what to do instead of actively negotiating. And for that they expect to be paid!!!

———

Ouch!! There is definitely a grain of truth to those complaints, maybe enough grain to make a loaf of bread.... And in many cases it's not really the buyer's agent's fault, but the fear of liability that keeps the agent from adding value, and sometimes it's just laziness or incompetence. As a buyer, they both look alike.

———

The hard part for agents is that we have several legal obligations and liabilities. First and foremost we have a legal obligation to only act in the interests and at the direction of our clients. So for instance, if you ask an agent to show you homes in a "nice neighborhood", your agent can't legally or ethically decide what a "nice neighborhood" is on your behalf, it's a fair housing violation, and interpreting and acting on that direction would open the agent up for discipline. So the agent needs the buyer to tell them what criteria the buyer has regarding location. Things like specific zip codes, specific neighborhoods or streets within those zip codes, specific school districts, etc... As a homebuyer you may choose to live where you like for your own reasons, but as an agent we cannot and will not assist someone in a way that leads to the agent doing something potentially discriminatory. And on top of that it would be terrible form for me as an agent to assume that a 75 yr old widow with a handicap parking sticker and a cane wants a condo in a 55+ community, when she may actually want 7 semi wooded acres to raise chickens, ducks, and goats. (True story - my mother bought just such a place at 75 after my father passed away). The key is that if your agent ISN'T making assumptions about what you want they are doing you a favor. I can sit down with you and let you build a custom search right in the MLS that fits every one of your wants and needs and send you an automatic email every time a home comes on the market that matches your search, you'll be notified of price increases, decreases, homes that come on the market, off the market, back on, etc... it gives you full control over your search and is part of what a good agent should do to partner with you during the process.

————

Second.... An agent cannot legally tell you what to bid on a particular home, and will not know what other clients are bidding (assuming it's a two agent transaction), and if it's a single agent, listing and buyer's agent, even though they likely know what other bids are the agent has a moral, ethical and legal obligation to keep that information confidential. Buyers want the inside info that will help them get what they want, especially after spending so much time with the realtor. However, if the listing agent is also working with you as a buyer, and they tell you how much to bid to win the home (assuming that the seller did NOT direct them to distribute that information to all buyers equally) how do you know that the agent is not just playing you to run up another bidder? The ethical stance in this situation is to advise you as a buyer to bid what you feel comfortable with both if you get the home AND if you don't get the home. IE a price where you don't feel you overpaid, and you won't regret not bidding higher. (In multiple bid situations this often happens in a "highest and best" round of bids).

———

So we've discussed a couple of ways that an agent CAN'T help you as a buyer, I think it's important to spend the rest of this section and discuss what we CAN do for you.

———

Buyer's agents are not limited to sending you the most recent updates to the MLS we can help you search for off market homes. One service that I perform for my buyers when needed is searching for homes for them that are not on the market. It's not unusual for me to be out walking a neighborhood on a Saturday morning hanging door flyers and talking to everyone in a neighborhood that my client is interested in moving into. Why? Because my client hasn't found the right home yet, and has a particular desire to move into a particular neighborhood or development. I'll door knock, hang flyers on doorknobs letting residents know I have a buyer and what the buyer is looking for, mail postcards, and make phone calls until I have either found a homeowner the is interested in selling or found out that there are no homes that will be coming on the market in that neighborhood anytime soon. I'll work with FSBO sellers, I'll do whatever it takes to make sure that I am giving my buyer the best service I possibly can. Do I do this for every single person that I've shown a home to? No, of course not... many people are using 10 different agents to look at 10 different houses and are working with agents as "door openers" not partners... but if I have a serious, qualified buyer who is working with me as their exclusive buyer's agent it's something that I regularly do.

Buyer's agents should provide comparable sales information prior to you making an offer. I just said above that as an agent I can't tell you what to bid. I can however, give you data that gives you an unbiased view of the market and an opinion on what a fair market value might be for the home. It may sound like splitting hairs, but understand the difference. Your agent can't tell you what to bid - that's steering you and might be for their own gain. An agent can and should tell you what recent sales in a neighborhood were and be able to tie that to what an expected selling price for the home you are looking at would be, then let you use your own judgement to decide if you would like to bid higher, lower, or around the suggested value. Many times my clients elect to bid lower, much lower, or even insultingly lower, higher, or almost exactly at the comp report value, and I happily submit those bids whatever they are because I am working FOR my client. In other words your agent can't tell you what to bid, but your agent can educate you on market conditions that will allow you as a buyer to make an intelligent, educated decision instead of an emotional one.

————

Buyer's agents also help to put you in touch with professionals that help you through the entire home buyer process. Experienced reputable agents often have several mortgage brokers, bankers, home inspectors, title companies, etc... that they have worked with in the past that the agent knows will help to make the process go smoothly. I personally have bank executives at well known banks that will answer my call at 7pm on a Sunday. I've had clients who have had problems in the mortgage process and have called a banker on Christmas day and gotten a call back with action because we have a relationship through working together that is friendly yet professional and the banker values my clients enough to take the call and do whatever he can to help them. Now do you think I recommend that particular banker to my clients after that? Of course I do! Not only did he save that particular client over $30K over the life of their mortgage he was able to move up the closing date over the holidays because the clients had a deadline to move that had changed. I never tell my clients who to use because that is their choice, I do recommend several options for mortgage, inspections etc... that I have worked with in the past that have treated my clients well. I get nothing out of the referrals other than protecting my clients. The point is that without a quality buyer's agent, you'll be flying blind in choosing inspectors, bankers, etc... and this can cost you significantly in added fees, poor service, or worse.

————

A quality buyer's agent should also take the time to understand your want's and needs. One thing I regularly do especially with higher priced properties is I give a wants and needs sheet to all decision makers - both partners if the buyer's are a couple, allow them to fill out the form and then we compare. A lot of times a husband and wife team may have significantly different opinions. I try to make sure that we find the common ground, concentrate on that, and allow them to direct me to which parts for each of them are must have's, nice to have's and dealbreakers. I am there to consult with them, and assist them in the most important decision in their lives at this moment and it is my job to listen an to consult, not just open doors.

———

A buyers agent after the transaction will help to keep you on track through the closing process. The closing process takes a LOT of work and this is the part that most agent's dislike because it's a lot of paperwork, details, negotiations over what inspections need done, when they're getting done, which items are worth repairing, what's a dealbreaker, what paperwork a bank is missing, what does the title agency need now?!!! Ok I think I just had a heart palpitation thinking about it!!! The point is most of this should be happening behind the scenes to keep you stress free and have the process be an enjoyable one. Your agent should be keeping you in the loop, but not stressed, handle the issues that come up that don't need your attention, and immediately bring to your attention the issues that do.

Chapter Ten

FINANCING CONSIDERATIONS

One of the things that a reputable realtor will ask you for prior to showing you homes or beginning negotiations on your behalf is a pre-qualification.

———

Pre-Qualification basically means that you have supplied your basic income and expenses information along with your credit history to a lender who will then tell you how much you are able to safely borrow on a new home. Some may even be willing to lock in an interest rate, or give you several options on financing.

———

Pre-Approval basically takes pre-qualification a step further and fine tunes it by having the buyer fill out a detailed loan application and provide the needed documentation to the bank. A pre-approval can usually be quickly turned into an approval upon the acceptance of your offer. Think of a pre-qualification as a high level overview of your finances and lend-ability, and a pre-approval as a detailed close look that will give you a precise answer based on a similar level of due diligence on the banks part to what they will use in their final underwriting of your loan.

————

So for a seller having a buyer with a pre-qualification submit an offer is a good thing. It gives the seller a reasonable confidence that you will be able to get a loan on their home if they accept your offer. However a buyer with a pre-approval has a significantly higher chance of being approved. This difference can be significant if you get into a multiple offer situation.

————

For my clients I recommend getting a pre-qualification prior to starting a new home search because that will give everyone involved confidence that you are looking at the right houses for you, but get it upgraded to a pre-approval prior to submitting an offer on a particular property if at all possible so that your offer will have the best chance of being accepted in the event that there is competition for the home.

————

————

There are several common types of mortgages available to homebuyers, this is a partial list of common types.

————

Conventional mortgages are the most common type of mortgage and typically offer the lowest interest rates and fees to a buyer. In order for a mortgage to be "conventional" the loan typically requires between a 10%-30% down payment in order to qualify. Conventional mortgages may also be "interest only" where the payment is only being made on the interest due and is not applied to the balance of the loan. In this type of loan you will often find a balloon payment after a set number of years after which the mortgage will need to be renewed or the home refinanced.

———

FHA Mortgage - this is a very popular type of mortgage often used by first time buyers. The advantage of an FHA loan is that it has a reduced down payment, often as low as 3.5% of the value of a home. So on a $100,000 home with a conventional mortgage a buyer would need up to $10,000 - $30,000 down, and with an FHA loan the buyer may qualify with as little as $3,500. FHA loans are also more tolerant of lower credit scores because they are federally insured.

———

VA Loans are available with as little as $0 down. VA loans are available to current and former members of the US armed services, and require a certificate of eligibility. The details of VA loans are too numerous to get into here, but know that if you are a current or former member of the military, check on your eligibility because often you can get special financing as a result.

———

USDA Rural Housing loans were created to create growth in specially designated rural areas. Check with your mortgage broker or on the USDA website for your eligibility and the areas in which this loan type can be used.

———

ARM or Adjustable Rate Mortgages generally start out with a low introductory interest rate, and will adjust with market conditions. Be extremely careful with these because of the unpredictability of future interest rates and the changes that they could have on your house payment. ARM's are on of the primary financing tools that got homeowners in trouble during the recession, because as interest rates rose homeowner's payments increased beyond the borrower's ability to pay.

———

203k rehab loans allow you to finance "fixer upper" types of homes that need repairs in order to qualify for more traditional loan types. With a rehab or construction loan you will have to get quotes on expected repairs, and the home must be projected to appraise for the full purchase price PLUS the expected repair cost AFTER the repairs are completed. In other words you don't want to overpay for the home or the repairs because the home will not be worth enough after repairs to justify the repairs. These loans are often used on HUD repossessed homes, and other bank owned foreclosures.

———

In the previous section we discussed down payment requirements on various types of mortgages..... However, what we are really talking about is the loan to value ratio. The loan to value ratio is simply stated as the amount of equity the buyer will have in the home vs the amount of the mortgage on the home at the date of purchase. In other words, if you are purchasing a home valued at $100,000 and the bank requires an 80% Loan to Value Ratio you will need to have at least $20,000 in equity at the time of purchase, meaning the bank will agree to loan at most $80,000 on an appraised value of $100,000.

———

Does this mean you absolutely need to put down $20,000? Not exactly! If the home you are purchasing appraises for more than the $100,000 purchase price you may need less of a down payment, and if it appraises for less than $100,000 you will need to make up the difference in cash.

———

For example:

- Sale price $100,000
- Appraisal $90,000
- With 80% LTV
- The bank will loan a maximum of $72,000 ($90,000 X 0.8)
- A buyer will need $28,000 down payment

———

- A second example:
- Sale price $100,000
- Appraisal $110,000

- With 80% LTV
- The bank will loan a maximum of $88,000 ($110,000 X 0.8)
- A buyer will need a $12,000 down payment

———

- As you can see, from a buyer's perspective it becomes extremely expensive to purchase a home that doesn't appraise for the full purchase price or more because if the buyer chooses to continue with the purchase of the home the buyer must spend more money up front in order to make up for the amount that the purchase price is over the appraised value of the home.

———

What kind of associated costs are you likely to see when applying for a mortgage?

———

While most buyers are expecting the ongoing costs of their mortgage that comprise the total payment including:

———

- Principal - this is the amount of your payment that reduces the balance on the loan
- Interest - this is the amount of your payment that the bank is charging you that does not reduce the balance on your loan
- Mortgage Insurance - this is an insurance plan

required on loans with less than 20% down payment. Once your loan reaches an LTV ratio of 80% you may be able to remove this depending on the terms of your specific mortgage

- Property taxes and Homeowner's insurance – Instead of the homeowner paying these costs on their own, mortgage companies typically collect the amortized amount of taxes and insurance as part of the regular mortgage payment and pay them on the homeowner's behalf.

Many homebuyers are caught off guard by the upfront fees that a lender will be likely to charge including:

———

- Origination fees – These are fees that a lender charges you for "originating" a loan. They can include appraisal, underwriting, application fees etc... when comparing loans take the total cost of origination fees into consideration.
- Points – points are a fee that you pay upfront to a lender often used to buy down interest rates to a lower %
- Third party closing costs – These are charges for third parties that the bank may have had to pay in order to underwrite the loan, such as appraisers, inspectors, etc...
- Taxes and government fees – These are fees that may be charged by your local, state, or federal government. They are generally not included in your mortgage, but will be disclosed if they are.

- Prepaid expenses and deposits - These are payments in advance towards expenses such as insurance, taxes, etc.... That the bank will need to pay on your behalf prior to you having made enough regular mortgage payments to cover the cost. If the lender calculates that you will have a shortfall they will require a prepaid fee to cover these expenses until your regular payments have accrued enough equity in your escrow account to pay these expenses.

Chapter Eleven

PREPARING A BID

When preparing an offer on a property a buyer will sign a "Purchase Agreement" which will constitute the terms of their offer. The seller will be presented the offer by their agent, and will have the opportunity to accept, reject or counter, the buyer's offer.

———

Prior to submitting an offer a realtor should have taken the time to present the buyer with comparable homes in the area and given the buyer enough information to make their own informed decision in regards to making an offer. It is important that the buyer understands the likely value that a bank appraiser will place on the property to make an informed offer. Offer too much and the home won't be able to secure financing, offer too little and the seller may not accept the offer.

———

Zillow estimates, and similar automated online services do not typically give an accurate estimate of the value that a home may be able to be borrowed against. When in doubt always have a qualified licensed appraiser give an opinion, however an experienced realtor has enough training, and experience to give a reasonable well informed estimate of a home's fair market value.

———

Prior to submitting an offer, make sure that you are ready to follow through. A buyer will likely need to have proof of funds / ability to borrow in order prior to submitting an offer. Please refer to the section on pre-approval for more information.

———

While each brokerage typically has its own standard Purchase agreement they will typically have several common elements.

- Identification of the buyer and seller by name
- Identification of the property including a legal description or permanent parcel number
- A description of the condition under which the buyer is offering to take possession of the property - often described as being "AS IS PRESENT PHYSICAL CONDITION" - meaning that the property cannot be significantly altered during the course of the contract.
- A list of appliances and fixtures that the buyer is requesting to be included with the sale. Common

items may be appliances, drapery, Central Air, Fireplace tools and doors, etc...

- An area to specify specific items that are NOT included - commonly appliances, window treatments, etc...
- Whether the offer is a primary or secondary offer - IE this a backup offer or not.
- The offered purchase price
- The amount that the buyer is placing into escrow in "earnest money" * earnest money is not a legal requirement in Ohio although it is extremely common
- The amount an type of financing being obtained by the buyer. IE Cash, FHA, conventional, VA
- The timeframe that the buyer has to apply and be approved for a loan
- The expected date of closing and change of possession
- Distribution of closing costs
- Contingencies for inspections and who is expected to pay for them. Typically General, Septic, water, well flow, radon, lead paint, insects, etc... are common inspection types depending on your location
- The allowed timeframes and remedies allowed after inspections are finished
- Any addenda - Property disclosures, VA, FHA, etc...
- Identification of the real estate agents representing each party
- Signature lines for buyer and seller.
- Supporting documents such as agency disclosure, proof of funds (cash, pre-approval, pre-qaualification)

———

Today, the paperwork and contracts for most residential real restate transactions are managed, signed, and stored online using services such as Dotloop or Docusign. The advantage of this is that purchase agreements, offers, closing documents, changes in contingencies, etc... can all be edited, signed, submitted, and shared with all parties instantly. Most of these services work not only on your computer, but you can sign paperwork on a tablet or phone from anywhere in the world. The days where your real estate agent had to come to your kitchen table, or you had to come to their office to physically sign documents is largely a thing of the past.

———

That being said, not every agent, and not every buyer or seller are comfortable with or able to use online document signing. While rare, it does still happen that one side of the transaction will insist on in person physical signatures. If this happens in your situation, be patient, everyone is working towards a common goal. Experienced realtors will do their best to accommodate all parties to the best of their abilities.

———

Many buyers feel that bidding significantly lower than a seller's asking price, a practice commonly referred to as "Lowballing" is a good buying strategy. In some cases - particularly with investors who are purchasing homes to fix and flip, this actually is a quality strategy. However if a buyer is bidding on a home that they actually want to purchase, lowballing often backfires by upsetting the seller enough that instead of negotiating with the buyer, the seller has an emotional reaction and refuses to consider other higher offers from the same buyer later.

———

Another way that lowballing has hurt many buyers is they sometimes cause a seller to "hold the offer" and use it as leverage to convince other buyers to raise their bids ensuring more money in the seller's pocket, however sometimes when lowballing a seller ends up selling the home for less than you were really willing to pay because the seller compared the buyer's lowball offer against a more reasonable offer and chose the more reasonable one without countering.

———

The bottom line is when lowballing always be prepared to walk away from a home and to lose out entirely if your offer is not accepted. And if you're selling a home don't be offended by lowball offers, simply use them as a starting point and make sure you are getting a fair offer for your property;.

———

When putting in an offer to purchase a property one of the frustrations a buyer faces is the seller counter offering, or rejecting an offer outright.

———

A counteroffer occurs when a buyer makes an offer that the seller does not want to accept on its face value under it's current terms. A seller may counteroffer based not only on price but on any provision within the original offer.

————

Common reasons a seller will counteroffer include:

- Asking for a higher price
- Change of closing date
- Change in terms of inspections or contingencies
- Change in terms of closing costs and other fees
- Change in property or fixtures which are to be included in the sale.

————

From a technical standpoint should a seller choose to counteroffer (consult your attorney for specific legalities in your jurisdiction) once the seller chooses to NOT accept a buyer's original offer and submit a counteroffer the buyer's original offer is now null and void and the buyer cannot go back and accept it. A Seller's counteroffer constitutes a BRAND NEW offer to a potential buyer that the BUYER can choose to accept the new offer, or submit another counteroffer.

————

That sounds kind of confusing, so explaining another way - a contract is made when there is an offer AND an acceptance which binds and encumbers both parties to it's terms. IE you offer to sell a house for $X, and a buyer agrees to purchase a house for $X. As long as you both agree to the exact same terms, and both sign the agreement you have a legally binding contract. If the person making the offer has signed the offer, the other person can accept it exactly as is by signing it and sending it back to the offeror, and the contract is in effect. However if the person changes any detail no matter how minor and sends it back the offeror can walk away, agree, or keep negotiating. There is no contract until both parties have agreed and signed the exact same terms and delivered the contracts back to the other in the agreed manner. (This used to be courier, mail, then fax, then email, now typically online signatures using something like dotloop or docusign) (Again consult your attorney for specifics).

———

So from a practical standpoint if a seller has an offer that the seller was willing to accept, but the seller wants to counter just to see if the buyer may be willing to pay more there is some risk in NOT accepting it because the buyer has the choice to walk away, counter offer again, or accept the counter offer. As a buyer, if a seller counteroffers with terms that the buyer would be willing to accept there is some risk in submitting an additional counteroffer to get better terms because the seller now has another chance to walk away.

———

Why would a seller or buyer walk away? It's possible the seller or buyer just has regrets, seller's or buyer's remorse, possibly another offer has come in to the seller, another property came on the market that the buyer is interested in, any random life event that can change the perception of either party can cause someone to walk away from a transaction that the party would have otherwise executed if the terms change because we are all human and lives and circumstances can and do change in an instant.

———

Sometimes when a house is priced aggressively for the market it will result in multiple offers from multiple buyers in a very short timeframe.

————

From a sellers perspective this is a very good thing because they can take their time and choose the offer that works best for them. This might mean that the seller chooses the highest priced offer, OR it may mean that they choose an offer with more security such as cash vs. Financing, a faster, or even slower closing date, or an offer without contingencies for things like inspections vs a more traditional offer. Basically the seller is in the position of choosing which offer to accept instead of negotiating with a single buyer the seller

————

Often if a seller gets a significant number of offers during a short enough period of time that there are multiple active offers on the table, the seller will request all bidders to enter a "Highest and Best Round".

————

If this happens the prospective buyers have a couple of options:

- Change their original bid in some way including raising the bid, removing contingencies, changing the financing to cash etc... in order to make their bid more likely to be choses by the seller.
- Stand on their original bid in it's current form and hope that the seller chooses their original bid

- Walk away and withdraw their bid.

———

Why would a rational buyer willingly raise their bid on a home that they already bid on? Well that depends on how badly the bidder wants the property, and what means the bidder has to make their offer stand out. My advice to buyers in this situation is to bid enough that you won't regret it if the home sells for $1 more than your offer, but low enough that you won't feel like you overpaid by $1. Essentially bid the amount that they will be happy with the outcome regardless of whether their offer is chosen or not.

———

Multiple biding situations are stressful for a buyer, but can be very profitable for a seller because of the fear of missing out that many buyers may have, and the tendency for them to bid higher in what amounts to a sealed bid silent auction allowing the home to sell quickly for it's fair market value.

Chapter Twelve

THE OFFER HAS BEEN ACCEPTED

Congratulations, your offer was accepted, you are now under contract..... What happens now?

———

Finding a property and negotiating the deal is only half of the battle. Once you have had your offer accepted several things will happen rather quickly, and much of this will require attention on your part.

———

- You will likely need to give a title company your earnest money. Many purchase agreements will have a provision for earnest money (this is not mandatory in all places but is customary in most) and there may be a time limit, or even a method of payment such as wire transfer or bank check specified to get the payment to your realtor or the title agency. If you skip this step the seller MAY have the ability to walk away from the agreement because you can be considered in breach of the contract.

- You will need to apply for financing and get a commitment from the bank - this is very time sensitive because it will be specified in the purchase agreement to be completed by a certain time limit AND the bank needs adequate time to fully execute the loan. This should be fairly easy if you are financing through the same bank or mortgage broker that you used for your pre-qualification or pre-approval. Typically a simple phone call or email sent to your banker will start the process and the banker or mortgage broker will work directly with you to get all of the information you need to satisfy their requirements.

- You will have to schedule inspections right away. In a typical purchase agreement there is a time limit specified to have inspections completed. Inspectors are busy and may need days or weeks notice in order to complete the inspection. Contract with a qualified inspector IMMEDIATELY to perform the inspections specified in your purchase agreement.

- If you are financing lender will usually schedule an appraisal of the property themselves because the primary purpose of the appraisal it to ensure that the bank is protected and that the amount borrowed on the property fits within the loan to value (LTV) ratio that fits the mortgage type you are using.

- The title company may need some additional documentation from you and will be keeping in touch with all parties during the closing process.

―――

Your realtor should be helping you through this process by coordinating with the various parties on your behalf when appropriate, and assisting you with negotiation of remedies to any material issues uncovered during inspections.

―――

―――

Congratulations, you have accepted a buyer's offer, you are now under contract..... What happens now?

―――

Finding a buyer and negotiating the deal is only half of the battle. Once you have accepted an offer several things will happen rather quickly, and much of this will require attention on your part.

―――

- You will have to make your property available for inspectors and appraisers. This is a time sensitive issue because there are specific timelines specified in the contract, as well as tight deadlines that the banks may have to hold onto in order to make sure that the loans are fully executed on time.
- You will receive notice through your realtor regarding any issues uncovered during inspection and will have the opportunity to negotiate remedies to the issues with the buyer if you choose.

- If you have agreed to make repairs based on an inspection you will have to hire contractors to perform the work (typically electric, plumbing, or carpenter) quickly to make the repairs and provide you with receipts to prove that the work was done by a qualified individual.
- The title company may need some additional documentation from you and will be keeping in touch with all parties during the closing process.

———

Your realtor should be helping you through this process by coordinating with the various parties on your behalf when appropriate, and assisting you with negotiation of remedies to any material issues uncovered during inspections. Overall this process is significantly less complicated on the seller's side but no less stressful.

———

When a property is actively for sale on the MLS and available to be shown, have offers submitted, and is unencumbered by being under contract it will show up as "Active". This signifies that the property is actively for sale and being marketed to buyers.

———

On the MLS once the property is under contract the listing will usually change from "Active" to "Contingent". It will stay in the "contingent" status until all contingencies in the purchase agreement have been met or released. Financing and inspections are usually the primary contingencies although sometimes contingencies for a buyer's home to sell, or other custom negotiated contingencies may also be present to satisfy the buyer, the municipality, or the FHA, VA, etc... It is uncommon but not unheard of for a home that is contingent to come back out of contract and go back on the market in "Active" status again if the buyer and seller could not agree on remediating items that were found by inspection, or if the lender found that the loan could not be underwritten for any reason. For this reason many sellers choose to keep marketing a property and allowing showings and solicit backup offers on a property while it is in it's contingent status.

———

Once the contingencies have been met or remediated, the status will change to "Pending". The pending status means that the home is under contract, and all contract terms have been met, and it is awaiting final approval by the bank and title company to close (title transfer to the new owner).

———

Once the title has transferred, the property is said to have closed, and the buyer will take possession and is the official new owner of the property.

Chapter Thirteen

PREPARING FOR YOUR MOVE

Preparing for a move is a stressful time. There are many things happing all at once, and for even the most organized among us, it can be one of the most stressful trying times. The key to a smooth, enjoyable, trouble free moving experience is planning.

———

I don't know about you, but I am not always the best planner when it comes to larger complicated projects like moving, so in order to help myself I create a checklist of things that need to be done, and that helps me keep on track and not overlook something important later on instead of falling victim to becoming overwhelmed, or getting sidetracked.

———

The key takeaways that I have learned after moving several times myself, and seeing and helping many family members, friends and clients move over the years is that the moves that go smoothly, have a few things in common.

———

1. **Planning**
2. Plan your move out in advance in order to make sure that when the big day comes you aren't running around in a panic, but instead are calm, cool, collected, and ready for the day.
3. **Adequate Help**
4. If you are moving with just yourself and your immediate family, have an army of friends, or have hired professional movers plan according to the amount of help and transportation that you have available. This is one time where more is almost always better. Make sure all of your helpers know when and where to be, what job they'll be doing, where they're going, and that they'll take good care of your belongings.
5. Having too much help is generally preferable to having not enough.
6. I've seen large houses packed up, boxed up, and loaded safely into a moving van by family and friends in just a few hours, an nobody is tired out at the end of the day.
7. On the other hand, I've seen people try to do too much with too little help where it could take the movers weeks of packing, loading, transporting, unloading etc... to get the job done.
8. **Positive Attitude**
9. Moving can and should be a fun, memorable, enjoyable experience. You're starting a new life in a new home, a fresh start that you'll

remember for the rest of your lives. This is a time to enjoy, even though there's stress and hard work ahead, find the fun in it, enjoy the time with your family and use it to bond with one another.

10. Years from now, you'll have many fond memories of starting your new life in your new home.

———

Pre-Moving Checklist

1-2 Months Before Move

———

•Create binder/folder for moving records (estimates, receipts, inventory lists, etc.)

•Plan your moving method (truck rental, hiring movers, etc) and get cost estimates

•See if your employer will provide moving expense benefits

•Research storage facilities if needed

•Schedule disconnection/connection of utilities at old and new place

•[ ] Phone [ ] Internet [ ] Cable [ ] Water [ ] Garbage [ ] Gas [ ] Electric

•Plan how you will move vehicles, plants, pets and valuables

•Plan how you will arrange furniture in the new place - use a floor plan or sketch

•Hold a garage sale, donate, sell, or trash unnecessary items

•Schedule transfer of records (medical, children in school, etc.)

•Get copies of any records needed (medical, dental, etc.)

•Acquire packing materials (boxes, tape, stuffing/padding, markers, etc.)

•Make any home repairs that you have committed to making

•Return borrowed, checked-out and rented items

•Get things back that you have lent out

•Start using up food you have stored so there is less to move

---

3-4 Weeks Before Move

•Finalize moving method and make necessary arrangements

•Begin packing non-essential items

•Label boxes by room and contents

•Separate valuable items to transport yourself - label as DO NOT MOVE

•Keep a box out for storing pieces, parts and essential tools that you will want

•to keep with you on move day - label as PARTS / DO NOT MOVE

•Create an inventory list of items and box contents, including serial numbers

•of major items - use this as an opportunity to update your home inventory

•Fill out a Change of Address form at a post office or online

•Provide important contacts with your new address:

•[ ] Employers [ ] Family & Friends [ ] Attorney [ ] Accountant [ ] Others

•Notify your insurance and credit card companies about change of address

•Cancel automated payment plans and local accounts/memberships if necessary

•Take your vehicle(s) in for a tune-up, especially if you are traveling very far

––––––––

1-2 Weeks Before Move

––––––––

•Continue packing and clean as you go

•Pack items separately that you will need right away at your new place

•Plan to take the day off for moving day

•Find useful things for your children to do - involve them as much as possible

•Find someone to help watch small children on move day

•Begin to pack your suitcases with clothes and personal items for the trip

•Reconfirm your method of moving with those involved

•Make sure your prescriptions are filled

•Empty out your safe deposit box, secure those items for safe travel

•Schedule cancellation of services for your old place

•[ ] Newspaper [ ] Housecleaning [ ] Lawn [ ] Pool [ ] Water Delivery

•Check your furniture for damages - note damages on your inventory

•Take furniture apart if necessary (desks, shelves, etc.)

•Make sure all paperwork for the old and new place is complete

•If traveling far, notify credit card company to prevent automated deactivation

•Get rid of flammables such as paint, propane, and gasoline

•Try and use up perishable food

––––––

2-4 Days Before Move

•Confirm all moving details and that you have necessary paperwork

•Make a schedule or action plan for the day of the move

•Plan when/how to pick up the truck (if rented)

•Prepare for the moving expenses (moving, food, lodging)

•Continue cleaning the house as you are packing

•Defrost your freezer and clean the fridge

•Make sure essential tools are handy (screwdrivers, wrench, pliers, tape, etc)

•Pack a bag for water bottles, pen/paper, snacks, documents, and essentials

•Set aside boxes/items that you are moving yourself (make sure you'll have room)

––––––

Moving Day

•Remove bedding and take apart beds

•Go early to pick up the truck if you rented one

•Take movers/helpers through the house to inform them of what to do

•Walk through the empty place to check for things left behind - look behind doors

•Leave your contact info for new residents to forward mail

•Take inventory before movers leave, sign bill of lading

•Make sure your movers have the correct new address

•Lock the windows and doors, turn off the lights

•Use a padlock to lock up a rented truck

•At your new place ...

•Verify utilities are working - especially power, water, heating, and cooling

•Perform an initial inspection, note all damages, take photographs if needed

•Clean the kitchen and vacuum as needed (especially where furniture will be going)

•Direct movers/helpers where to put things

•Offer drinks and snacks, especially if the helpers are volunteers

•Assemble beds with bedding

•Begin unpacking, starting with kitchen, bathroom and other essentials

––––––––

Moving In - Weeks 1-2

•Check for damages while unpacking - be aware of deadline for insurance claims

•Replace locks if necessary and make at least 2 copies of your new keys

•Confirm that mail is now arriving at your new address

•Make sure your previous utilities have been paid for and canceled

•Complete your change of address checklist

•[ ] Bank(s) [ ] Credit Cards [ ] IRS [ ] Loans [ ] Insurance [ ] Pension plans

•[ ] Attorney [ ] Accountant [ ] Physicians [ ] Family support

•[ ] Newspapers [ ] Magazines [ ] Licenses [ ] Memberships

•Schedule a time to get a local driving license and update vehicle registration

•Get local phonebooks and maps

•Find new doctors, dentists, etc, depending on your needs & insurance

•After you are moved in, update your home inventory, including photos of rooms

•Update your renters insurance or homeowners insurance if needed

* This list was created by www.vertex42.com

You can get a free downloadable / Printable version of this form at:

https://www.vertex42.com/ExcelTemplates/moving-checklist.html

————

One of the most stressful parts of moving for many people is hiring a mover. For those of us who don't have a large family, or a dozen buddies to round up to move us for free, or we are relocating over a long distance it can be a necessity. Still, hiring a mover ranks right up there with going to the dentist and buying a car because it's something that most of us don't do often enough to develop a real comfort level with the process, and lets face it, if you only hire a mover once every 5-10 years and the mover moves someone every day..... Well they're at an advantage when it comes to negotiating, pricing, service, etc... and most of us will never know whether we got a good deal, a bad deal or a fair deal.

————

A few tips for hiring a mover are:

1. Check references / Reviews online. In today's world bad service brings bad reviews online. If a company is well established and has consistently positive reviews over a variety of social media like yelp, google, facebook, etc.... That can be a good indication that the company ie reputable. Ask to speak with someone who has recently used their services and get their opinion on how they were treated.

2. Before hiring the company get multiple quotes and let each company know that you are doing it. They'll be more likely to give you their best pricing upfront knowing that there is competition.

3. When getting quotes, make sure that the companies have all done a walkthrough and have done an inventory of your belongings. You want accurate quotes with no surprises, in writing so that you can compare apples to apples.

4. Deposits - most reputable companies won't require a large up front deposit. You will be charged after delivery, and when you are satisfied with the service the mover has provided.

5. Packing costs - One large swing in cost can be

determined by who is packing your belongings. You? Or the movers? One place where pricing can go up quickly is when the movers are responsible for packing your belongings for you. You may be paying inflated prices for packing supplies and labor. On the other hand, the moving company has experience packing items safely, and may be responsible for damages if they have packed your items instead of you.

6. Check your contract for extra fees, moving and delivery dates, uncharges, etc... that aren't obvious in the pricing provided. Comparing multiple quotes? Look for the fine print too.

7. Is your estimate binding? Guaranteed? Or Non Binding to Exceed? Make sure you read to know if your costs can go higher than you agreed to.

8. Are your items insured? At what value? And under what conditions? Make sure you know what the moving company is insuring you for, and what isn't covered before you choose your provider.

———

Don't be afraid of the process, just go in with your eyes open so that you are an educated customer. The vast majority of moving companies are reputable, and are going to take fantastic care of you an your belongings. But as with any major decision, do your homework and make sure you know who you are dealing with in advance.